Akashic Records

Master Your Life and Raise Your Vibration

(How to Understand the Akashic Records, Hear the Story of Your Soul and Connect With Divine Knowing)

William Davis

Published By **Jordan Levy**

William Davis

Akashic Records: Master Your Life and Raise Your Vibration (How to Understand the Akashic Records, Hear the Story of Your Soul and Connect With Divine Knowing)

ISBN 978-1-998038-61-9

No part of this guidebook shall be reproduced in any form without permission in writing from the publisher except in the case of brief quotations embodied in critical articles or reviews.

Legal & Disclaimer

The information contained in this book is not designed to replace or take the place of any form of medicine or professional medical advice. The information in this book has been provided for educational & entertainment purposes only.

The information contained in this book has been compiled from sources deemed reliable, and it is accurate to the best of the Author's knowledge; however, the Author cannot guarantee its accuracy and validity and cannot be held liable for any errors or omissions. Changes are periodically made to this book. You must consult your doctor or get professional medical advice before using any of the suggested remedies, techniques, or information in this book.

Table Of Contents

Chapter 1: Apply for permission

I can't stress it enough Do not look into anyone's Akshic files without permission. Certain readers may be able to access it via writing. It's not necessarily a bad thing however, I think it's is a bit overkill. Just ask them for the permission of their spouses to access their documents and nothing other than their. They are not their husbands. They don't have children. They don't have wives, mothers parents, uncles and old friends ... just their own. You will surely encounter many instances in which they interact with one another. Most of the time, the client may meet someone else on their own record and it is your responsibility to look over the records and then explain the situation. Then, you must explain to them the reason this particular relationship occurred. It is important to explain how they should have learned about, and then what they didn't understand and the reason they are being forced to repeat the same mistake... over and repeatedly. That's as far as it gets. You don't read any further about the person's connection to the other. There is nothing related to the person's documents because they do not have any relevance to the individual that you're reading about. The ethical issue is not to take it further.

You should ask the person you're studying to give the full name of their family; every name they have, including divorced names, maiden names names, foster names named stage names, adopted names, and legally altered names. Every one of these has Karma associated with them, and as a result, they each have their own history or at the least one or two chapters in the text.

Yes, it's difficult. The akashic record and your family karma doesn't end in your family of origin just because you're adopted. Your family is still a in the same family as your parents and have ancestral the DNA and ancestors to that family, whether you like you or not. In addition, you are part of the akashic record of your new family, as well as their fallout from karmic events and relatives. If it's through marriage, adoption or another reason you might have multiple family members, we share relationships and bonds to greater numbers of people than we think. The step parents of the couple, brothers and sisters or cousins who are who are 10 times removed, all of the family members of the 3rd, 2nd, 4th, and on. These bonds and ties will not always disappear in the event of divorces or deaths. It is true that we all are connected to each other, and just as everyone else; we have a difficult time understanding the people we're connected to, what the depth of these connections are, or even what the reasons we're connected at all in the first place.

Chapter 2: It's All About The Energy

Everything. Everything is energy. The chair looks like one, however, it's actually energy. It appears to be an old brick structure, however it's actually energy. If it's energy, it is able to be detected.

Every building has a history and their own energy, which is why buildings come with an akashic track record.

In other words, everyone who has worked in a building is left with a little energy that they have left inside the building. This could be read in isolation or merged into a brand new character and interpreted in a collective. Did the building come into existence from the moment it was imagined by someone else's thoughts? It was born as it was designed on plans? Was it created when it was first put in place? Was it created when the final brick laid? Most of the time, structures or houses remain vacant for years due to of the energy associated with it, or their location. Many lives lost in the construction process will leave marks due to the energy removed or produced.

Recently, I was able to take an exclusive tour through the building that is haunted here located in San Antonio dating back to the year 1870. I have firsthand knowledge about the residual energy of those who passed away there, or were murdered there, as well as a local person who was confused as the place he died at the spot prior to when San Antonio was even a real city. The building's owners weren't aware of the fact that they had built over the site in which his body was buried however, he did for some reason decided to remain in the area, leaving his imprint over the spot for ever.

Furniture functions exactly the identical. Make sure you wash the antiques well before you bring them inside your house.

They also have energy and you don't wish to have any unidentified energies hanging around with you. If you're doubtful, consult the nearby Shaman or priest take care of the piece or use an akashic record psychic to discover what the significance of the object is. Family heirlooms are full of power. They've witnessed disputes, love and divorces, marriages violent acts, murder, deaths, births and everything else in between. This energy gets encased in the item and has to be cleaned prior to install it in your child's room, or in any other space within your house. Things you purchase at the thrift shop are similar, but they're likely to come from a person's energy and should be at the very least salted and aged prior to use.

However, your food items aren't completely safe. The food items are constantly being touched by people and canned items carts, food items, and other things at the grocery store. This is the reason it's good to scrub not only your fruits and veggies, but also your meats, canned products and other items are best rinsed in cold water prior to cooking/consuming the food items. Restaurant servers and cooks could affect the flavor of food according to the mood they're at the time they serve your food. If the cooks have trouble or fighting, it could make things difficult for not only those around them however, the food picked the energy of those around them as well. If the cook is just falling in love with you, the food might seem more appealing during a period of time.

There is something to consider The real reason why that we bless and pray for the food we consume before eating it is not simply give thanks, but also to alleviate the suffering of the energy that the animals experienced when they gave its life to us.

This energy isn't an ingredient we must consume.

Animals both domestic and wild animals have akashic records. Autos also have an akashic record. The paintings have records of akashic especially portraits and images which can both be read. However, I'm guessing that you'll be looking to learn about people or their pets. Perhaps just for you. Whatever the case, the chapters that follow will provide you with an explanation of what you should do, and what you should not do, details on background and guide on how to get access to libraries and the best ways to use the library's resources.

Chapter 3: Self Care and Protection

It is vital to take care of both physically and mentally. Stay well rested, healthy and maintain a balance throughout everything. However sometimes, I've gone into the astral realm when I was tired and hungry. I was able to get an accurate reading. However, it's best to be alert and refreshed.

Be sure to surround yourself every moment with light and love. In particular, when traveling to the astral plane or the akashic plane. The things hanging in the air will be pleasant. There are some entities that be aware of your presence and attempt to grab hold of you and chase your home. It is for this reason that you must pray for protection whenever you do any type or work in another realm of existence. It's not only Akashic Records; even when praying or meditation, you're on a totally higher plane or a non-ordinary state which is why you must make sure that you're protected. When I refer to the existence of a new plane numerous metaphysicians (also called spiritual or woo folks) will refer to this as a different state of being to differentiate from the ordinary waking state. It is also a different condition or an entirely different level of existence.

In particular, I'm quoting myself in my post, when I mention

"I know that I am surrounded by God's loving healing protective light and nothing that can harm me can enter into this Sacred Space. Nothing harmful can attach itself to me. My guides and angels protect me and support me. Nothing harmful can follow me home. I am always safe."

Do not leave any room for doubt the fact that your prayers are effective with full power every moment. It's not that they'll work in the future, but you're certain you are praying for success, or you just kind of believe it there is a chance, or that you're pretty certain God is a good God and will protect your life even if you might not merit it. I will say strongly that there is no place for this kind of thought. Such a wishy-washy mindset could lead to your being killed or taken over, or even worse, the guides you trust may allow you to proceed even if they are aware that you're not prepared. Guides will generally protect yourself from harming yourself however, they may not always. Someone who is arrogant and determined who lacks faith, discipline or faith can plunge straight into the bottom of the abyss despite their guides' best efforts. Sometimes (yes I can relate to my own experience which was extremely costly) they leave you alone and live your life the way they want it. It's never a good idea.

You should be positive and certain of your capabilities and in the angels, guides and ancestral ancestors' abilities to guard your interests. It is here that training comes into play and, in the end, will pay off spectacularly.

You must be able to demonstrate faith in and trusting your mentors. It is built on trust through duration as you become meet each other just like any relationship ought to.

Chapter 4: Re-incarnation

There is no way to discuss previous lives without mentioning the possibility of reincarnation. It's identical. Some people don't consider reincarnation a possibility and this is fine.

Reincarnation is the cycle of birth, death, and rebirth. The entire purpose of reincarnation is to allow the soul to grow to eventually join with the Divine/God, or to ascend into the next level.

There are so many things to be learnt, numerous experiences that you can have that just a couple of days are not enough. the soul must have an additional lifetime in order for this reconnection. When compared to the Divine Our life span can be a flash before we're out of the picture. The soul requires more than just one individual or even a single day can provide it.

When this one life ends The soul continues for another life. Each existence is etched on the soul. Experiences that were learned, or lessons not learnt, hurt fear, love wishes, fears and so on are carried on. The moment a soul through the guidance of guides, determines the important life lessons needed and even the other souls require the same, it chooses either parents or families that we can return to. This is typically with souls that we know or with karma we can deal with.

The reason we come back is varied, however, we always return for soul's growth. It is true that the persona is extremely significant and it is possible for the personality to actually derail the soul's goal. It's an amazing experience to be human, and your soul may become lost in the moment and especially in the early years of a person's life.

The most common way to tell if you have an aspiring young man or woman because of their lack of fundamental capabilities. Most of them do not have the ability to comprehend things in life. Many things, particularly mechanical ones are confusing to their minds. For them, they "don't get it" and may feel lost and disorientated within the ocean of daily life. It is possible that they are stressed and require ongoing therapy. They may not be at ease in their skin and might be looking for ways of getting out of this tangled and traumatic life. It is also possible that they not belong to this realm or perhaps this is their first experience as a person from Earth. There are numerous possible scenarios that it is impossible to explore them all in a single life-time.

On the other hand, an older soul seems to be taking a holiday. They don't have a lot of needs and appear to be able to comprehend the ways in which life operates. They do need to be taught however, they'll be more able to instruct than to learn.

Begin by asking questions about the pre-birth contract, vows, and oaths made or taken in another lifetime. These are where some positive and negative patterns in our lives are derived from. Conditions under which we, or more specifically our soul, in the past time incarnation took the vows/oaths are now obsolete, but the soul carries them along to the present and our personality remains to these beliefs. Soul, it appears is able to set up family members and experience to help with its learning and teaching while we remain with no guidance to figure to resolve the problems or issues that we face and to get better.

We often encounter relationships in which we're victimized, abused or exploited or even worse. There are times when we take poor paying jobs due to the need to survive. We are not loved due to the belief that we are inadequate because of a past existence, we have been beaten and believed in the lies that we were told by others. We simply didn't have the wisdom of our times however, we must nevertheless be cured in order to grow or change as the soul takes the belief that it holds and this belief is the reason that the individual has to contend with.

Naturally, it doesn't need to be that way Many people are motivated by the desire to make a mark in business, or eliminate injustice in society as well as to be in giving back.

In any case, we are being born to specific types of people, and in particular kind of situations, and we tend to be surrounded by those of the same kind Our soul family like it or not. The merry-go around continues until we finally and all understand the lessons that we agreed to as well as learn to love unconditionally and non-judgment, then we are able to rest at the feet that is the Divine or rise into the next level. There is lots of work to complete and a lot of healing to come through.

Chapter 5: Before You Even Begin

Prior to stepping foot in any of the universes be aware of the things you observe and experience. Any thing can be very meaningful. What kind of birds do that you spot flying on the ground or on the ground, the hue of grass, stones that line the sidewalk and the different types of trees, colors of buildings, and even the teachers and librarians that show up can mean something Are they younger? Old? Are they like they are familiar? Are they willing to give suggestions?

Be aware of any objects that appear to leap into your view. Perhaps within the next few hours or two of your everyday routine that you come across an object that is just like it. This is not only a blessing by Spirit but a proof that you weren't just dreaming about something. I suggest you get an encyclopedia on symbols and archetypal interpretations. Simple and not overly academic, you don't need to stress your life any more than you already are. One of the best books for understanding animals includes "Animal Speak" by Ted Andrews. I have a copy the book and read frequently. It's been extremely useful in deciphering messages from my guides, and spirits all over the world. Animals from other realms are excellent indicator of where you're along your path. They can also teach you things you should learn as well as a hint at what kind of people you will meet on the planet of humanity.

Avoid picking up any object you see; simply note its form, color or size, and the other details that appear significant to you. Don't attempt to take something back. Don't accept anything that is offered to you unless absolutely certain that it comes directly from your spirit guidance. If you are not sure, think about it numerous times. It is a fact that I can't stress enough.

If your spiritual guides are offering you something, the gift will be manifested on the surface of your day within a few days. Don't try to return anything. This could be a trap or trick of a less than friendly spirit or perhaps a trickster spirit.

Only one exception to this is if you are a teacher or librarian at the library hand you a book. You might accept it since it is not something you will be bringing to home, instead and you're reading it as you're at the library and handing it back at the request of the librarian. Be careful not to ruin the book by making marks on it, rings on pages, or cutting away pages. It's like seeing an axe-wielding, raging madman who is chasing you from front to back to get an old bookmark or piece of paper.

Chapter 6: The Lower, Middle & Upper Worlds

The realms of the lower levels are used for a myriad of reasons and are similar to our brains. They are usually less luminous or darker visually than the normal humans, and are always in darkness. It's a great area and it is often in the area where you will get to meet your animal spirits or animals totems. Some traditions suggest that souls are lost and have to be brought back. The lower realm is alike to the astral plane, and utilized in the exact same manner, however it is used more so when it is used for subconscious or higher working, however this only scratched only the top of what lower-levels mean and the ways they function. I wouldn't recommend working on these levels because there are numerous hazards and traps to avoid. You might need to revisit to avoid, or get help to return from the levels. The levels aren't unfriendly however, they are just like other areas in everyday life they are not the ideal location to be stuck with out the help of a lifeline.

The world of the middle from a shamanic viewpoint is a lot like our everyday one. Just like being slightly out of sync, and in pure energy and possibilities where everything is feasible. This is where we usually visit when doing guided meditations, as well as the lower level of astral travel and the initial step to the other dimensions of the universe.

The higher world, also known as the middle astral, or the universes that are just over ours are also referred to as the akashic plane, or field. It's brighter than the reality we experience on a regular basis. It is also where a variety of items and people are located, and not only in the library. This is those we visit whenever we experience experiences that are out of body such as a near-death experience, or when our guides visit us when we're asleep to study or discover new ideas and concepts. There have been reports from people feeling that they were on some sort of college or school campus. The perception of time has been altered, they believed that it was hours, when it was actually just minutes that passed by on the street.

Many who have experienced near-death experiences are reporting similar times of distortion. My old school teacher was DOA in the emergency room following a massive automobile accident. With a lot of devotion from staff members, the teacher was able to get through. He claimed he'd gone to the darkness, and had was able to spend a few months in the company of the ascended masters, learning things that was beyond his memory (his soul was able to remember it however, as I'm certain) after which he was returned to the light only to wake up to the defibrillator as well as a needle that was swollen with adrenaline. On a related note He was unhappy. He wanted to remain in school. He was very content at the same time.

I'm sure that you've had the pleasure of hearing about astral travel which is the location we travel to when we escape from this earth into the realms above. When you take a moment to examine your surroundings and look around, you'll see churches, schools, and many other items you are familiar with. Astral is the most direct representation of the world we live in, and therefore, it's the one that we most associate with.

There are several realms that are above the astral, but it is necessary to master how to traverse each level first, and this requires lots of time and meditation, this isn't something I'm prepared to tackle in this book.

Chapter 7: Special Tools & Guides

It is not necessary to have anything special apart from your thoughts, your intentions and hands. However you can use some methods and devices that may help you when you are working.

Sage was used over the centuries by Native Americans for cleansing their houses, sacred instruments and their minds, bodies and minds, etc. Sage also contains anti-bacterial as well as anti-viral and anti-fungal properties, just like most of the herbal remedies for cleansing. It is recommended to clean your surroundings and yourself by using sage or possibly sweet grass or lavender. You might want to add salt or water to the list of tricks to cleanse. Salt acts as a preservative, and assists in keeping your home clean and neat. Make sure you don't apply salt-based water to furniture fabrics as when drying, it leaves tiny white marks on all surfaces. Sage is essential for maintaining your home and individual free of attachments. The rest are those supporting elements that provide uniqueness to the overall mix. An internet-based search can provide some excellent results. Attachments are spots or locations inside or on the body of the energy field of your body, in which entities can grab hold of you and follow you back across the barrier. Do not wish that never.

A crystal's hold could help you stay secure, and help you focus the mind and act as a wand, particularly in the event that you envision the crystal being carried by you towards the astral. Try it out in your head and observe the type of connection you could establish with the crystal as well as the ways it will work for you. Crystals are living entities and not in the way they appear to be, but live consciousness is still. Speak to them, inquire about them.

Discuss with them the most effective way to interact or collaborate together. Certain types of crystals are ideal for specific purposes. To protect yourself, use smoky quartz and amethyst. Black tourmaline, or whatever you are confident with. It will give you some protection. Clear quartz is always a good all-purpose crystal.

An eye-catching candle may be beneficial to set up ahead of time and the shade of the candle might have meaning for you. White is the best color as it symbolizes pure intent. Pink represents the unconditional love of or towards self. The color green represents growth or healing. It might even be the meadow or a pleasure. Blue could symbolize the ocean, a lake or another body of water in case you are drawn by the symbolism. An investigation into the colors of candles and their meanings could be helpful, but generally speaking, white serves a intended to represent the Godhead as well as the angels. As you embark on the journey, you should close your eyes and concentrate on your inner self and the direction that will appear ahead of you.

If you're tempted to try a pendulum, make sure you understand how to operate it prior to you even begin. Pendulums aren't just instruments that can be used to answer yes or no. They are much more than this and I don't suggest using them for the work of akashic records because they distract you from the task at hand and instead focus on the pendulum. If you do feel it is necessary to have the pendulum direct you to the direction of the library do so, however it is not possible to bring the real pendulum along with you, so you'll need to master how to use the spirit of the pendulum within the akashic level. It is necessary to understand its spirit, however this is a whole new degree.

You can ask the librarian to access it in the library, however as I've seen, that the librarian will hand to you the books you request to borrow. They don't want that you to wander around by yourself. I'm sure of it. I've attempted. I failed.

If you are more at ease being guided by your GateKeeper or guardian angel, or any saint, don't hesitate to reach their assistance or advice. They'll never be disappointed and remain with you for as when you require them to be. If you're comfortable with your animal or totems, request assistance from them. If they are unfamiliar with them. But don't attempt to do it now. It is essential to understand and comprehend them prior to working on them. The group you work with could appear to be a soft, cuddly bear to you but to another person they may appear to be a huge Grinch with claws that measure 10 inches waiting to strike should they break your heart. A careful consideration of whom you bring along with you is essential. Although I have to say that at this point, I've not discovered anything on the astral which made me feel like I was at risk. I've always felt secure. Naturally, I feel this as a normal humans as well. There's no need for anyone to worry about me. I'm not a victim, nor am I carrying the mindset of a victim within my own energy area. I am part of. I am confident in my appearance. I am not a part of the crowd or make a statement. I'm confident about my own place and within the world, and I am not a target for anyone regardless of where I am. This means that I am not in reason to bring my animal companion with me except for an excursion. This isn't to say that, if I had that I needed to, I wouldn't summon the Arch Angel Michael. I'd call upon Michael and his sword to defend me immediately.

Based on Keith Meadows in his book, The Shamanic Experience,

"A power animal is the expression in the animal body of a capacity to accomplish the task. It's an energy pattern in the unconscious and subconscious that was created by the Human Spirit. Also the animal shape embodies the characteristics, traits and behaviors of a primarily spiritual energy that is the capacity to do specific tasks and then allow it to manifest in the material reality.

The power animal therefore is an energy pattern of the powers that it embodies.

The qualities and traits mentioned above aren't the characteristics of one particular animal, nor the idealized group soul of the entire animal species its echoes inside one's body of energy, but rather constitute a part of individual human character. It's the force of life that is embodied in the archetypal animal, and has the ability to manifest through human language. Thus, although a powerful animal is able to possess all the characteristics that is its Earth animal cousin It is also a source of both physical and mental power that is able to be expressed in human terms. When connecting to this energy source, you can tap into its unique characteristics."

Therefore, unless you are certain that your animal of choice is adorable and innocent fuzzy rabbit take it off to a different time and location. In my previous post, the only thing you require is the strength of your intentions and mental ability to go wherever that you wish to visit in the universe.

Maintain your calm mind. It isn't the right time to be panicking. What ever you experience or hear, you should not get scared; simply walk to your left slowly, or walk in case you feel scared. Don't get caught up in the situation. It is always possible to get your mind off the sand and go back to your place in the world of humans and not ever go back, even if not wish to. You can also regroup to try again using more defense, greater determination and self-confidence.

Chapter 8: Why Are You Afraid of the Water?

It is possible you've had a terrible experience on the beach while you were an infant. Maybe you've ever seen a massive pool of water before, which scares you. Maybe you've been drowned by a ship in a previous life, or eaten by sharks. Or maybe you fell from an cliff for a human sacrifice. There are a variety of causes that have nothing related to your experience during this lifetime.

The belief is birth defects as well as unproved moles or scars and strange spots within your body, where injuries were sustained that might have resulted in your death fighting in another life. There is a chance that the birth defect you have was handed to you as a learning experience that you had to master because of certain behaviors that you witnessed or forced on other people during a previous life.

Insane fears, extreme behavior that include a high degree of distrust of people around you or the tendency to use as hypochondria, a front-line sitter and even an excessive motivation to achieve is a remnant from an earlier existence. It's not necessarily good thing. Many individuals are motivated to overcome social problems because of the experiences they had in their previous lives. It is my opinion to consider Mother Teresa as one of the people who are driven.

Think about the reasons that you're experiencing certain behavior or habits. If you don't have a reason for them in your current life, this is probably something you have brought with you as well as a lesson that you've to overcome or learn. What is it that you are always putting off or refusing to meet people who are your friends? How come you keep trying to remain invisibly invisible? What is it that makes you being so independent? Do you ever refuse aid? Do you have a reason to always ask for assistance, feeling like you can't do it on your own feet, and that you need someone else take care of you?

Do you see the way this works? It's a pattern which with every lifetime, we have a opportunity to break. If we don't know what caused the issue, it's often hard and if not impossible to solve. We ride on the merry-go-round for a lifetime after another, through the years in a state of ignorance of despair, anxiety and longing, or even flounder through life with no worry.

It is now more crucial than ever to know the story of your journey through the soul, the best way to get it and solve the issue in a single, comprehensive way to ensure that we don't need to bear the burden of the practices we created to our own lives. There is a need to go through to understand what motivated us to sign the agreements as well as the promises we made, so that could finally be able to fulfill them or change them once and forever and let ourselves go. To take a new path and allow the past to be the past, we have to travel through the rabbit hole to find the answers.

The time is getting shorter for our current generation to come together. New paradigms are emerging and our world is changing quicker than any of us could have anticipated. It is imperative that we adapt to the challenges or else our soul could be sucked away or worse...start all over again.

Chapter 9: Meeting Up With Yourself

What will you discover in your personal book? What can the chapter's chapters tell you about yourself? were in the past? In what way will this relate to what you're currently? Do you enjoy the things you are seeing? What do you think of the information? Do you consider yourself a good human being or an opportunistic barbarian? Yes, everyone has been a mass killer and saint. There have been many times that we returned life to witness how it feels to be on both aspects of an issue, to witness what it's as a pure sinner as well as to feel the joy of become the light, and to experience all of the things that lies between.

Don't be surprised when you look around It is just the way of the world, as it should be. Also, it means that you need to improve your skills and plenty of forgiveness you can seek from people around you. Before you can seek forgiveness from other people, you have to first get it within yourself.

Understanding that we are operating within a specific amount of knowledge. We know things that was not known just three years ago, and even just a few hours ago. We don't know what we'll be able to comprehend in the future. So, you can't hold yourself today to the same standards that you might face in the near future. You certainly can't hold yourself to standards that you didn't have before.

It is impossible to fully comprehend the various forces that playing in the creation of people like Hitler. The root of the problem was more than a single twisted brain. It was a cosmic force in play that could remain hidden until we achieve the full ascension, or reunification with God/Creator.

I am bringing this issue up to remind you not to be a victim of your actions that were not in line with whom you once were. Perhaps you've played a role in a larger scheme. You must forgive yourself on a spiritual level, and others will do the same. The same way, make sure you offer forgiveness to yourself for the wrongs you have done previously. Refraining from forgiveness means to stop someone else's progress toward ascending. This also means you remain tied to them, and to the anger and hurt. It is really beneficial to let your mind relax, ease the hurt and then move on to an entirely new direction.

The act of forgiveness is an important way to ascend ourselves. In letting go of the hurt and hurt is to start living. It's not about an enormous scale and not just about the guy who slashed you at the intersection. Your in-laws who attempted to end your relationship, the colleague who snatched up your promotion that person who sexually assaulted when you were a kid; In each case, forgiveness has to be made on a variety of different levels. For allowing you to be used, or not having the courage to voice your opinion to begin with or for someone else because they did not believe in the story, or for insanity as well as lack of compassion as well as their own fears and possibly self-loathing.

Unforgiveness keeps us attached to an individual or event and causes us to be angry. It creates ulcers, and hinders the spiritual development of our children. This shrieks of the need to get justice, the desire to prove right, and the need for publicly lauded, and the right to dance through the streets in awe. It is rare to receive this type of acknowledgement from any person.

Chapter 10: Healing Across the Timelines

The ability to overcome the past and make a new beginning. The practice of meditation, sending healing energy or observing the past/future remotely isn't just a possibility, it is used daily to help heal people and situations from the past. It is also possible to use this technique to identify pivotal points in your life's journey in which decisions are re-examined to allow for quicker and complete healing. It is said that hindsight can be 20/20. ideal for this kind of healing.

Here's a technique I have used not only for my clients, but also with myself. The subconscious mind can't discern between what's happening or even what's memories. Due to this small flaw of the brain, we have the ability to go back to our experiences in the previous lives and make changes to the past. As an example, I was a victim of bullying when I was a kid and, as a consequence, I had an intense fear of public situations as well as being with other people. I avoided social situations as much as I could and did not walk alongside other children. I was the only one to eat in the cafeteria but rarely talked to anyone.

In my adulthood, this kind of behavior was very painful. I sat in my the meditation room to help my child inside me. I reverted to my memories and stood beside the person I used to have been and encouraged her to assert her self. I gave my own child encouragement and positive words and affirmations. I helped her see that those who have criticized her had a jealousy and were petty. I helped my own younger self see that their comments were just lies.

Since the subconscious mind is very flexible it was possible for me to have a major impression. In the course of a single night, I needed to continue doing the task and until this very day I go to my younger self in order to offer advice, give pep talks, occasionally I treat her to an ice cream.

This method even helped me to re-invent myself following the finality of a very long and messy breakup. I altered my conversation with my ex to defend myself better and to re-form the memories. I came out more confident and had my perception of worth a greater result. You can too.

Chapter 11: Why Do We Keep Doing This

As of this moment, I am blessed to have a close acquaintance, Della Fannette Williamson. Della has been involved in past lifetime work well before I started and was aware of certain connections between us as we first came into contact. In her memoir "My Life as Past Lives of an Ordinary Woman" she recounts a period in Egypt when she was an infant girl who was preparing to become the temple priestess.

My name is Issi. I am from what is now called Egypt.

My understanding of the world is a bit limited. My universe is tiny and cozy. I'm happy in my understanding of it.

I am living in the days prior to the time when Egypt was referred to as this it was an era of simplicity as it appears to me. It is a time when people are more in touch with the divine illumination of God. Gods than any other point in time. We do not know this.

I recall being entrusted to the priestesses of Isis at the age of a child by my parent. My parents were followers of all Gods however they were compelled to join me in Isis. They believed that I was born with a mark that indicated I would become an Isis follower, student as well as a Priestess Isis.

They probably meant to refer to the bizarre birthmark I have in my stomach. It's kind of like the eyes of Isis when you look closely. However, people only see the things they wish to perceive.

I was raised in the tender care and love that the Priestesses had of Isis. There was more than one person who was there. The other girls are given to Priestesses in order to master the art of Isis. Our lives are filled with joy and love for one another. We have responsibilities. enjoyed freedom and love each other like the sisters we are. We're not slaves. We love and, at the very least, can do what we are doing, which is learning about the nuances of our Sisterhood. Certain of us are destined to join the Sisterhood of Silence and some are destined to become Priestesses. What we'll be will be decided after that we've learned and experienced the teachings of Isis. The most enjoyable part of my time of learning is the full moon, when we can all pray together and then bathe in the river till dawn to commemorate Isis taking a bath following her struggle with Seti. It's a great feeling.

There are those who join members of the Sisterhood of Silence. It is a distinct group inside the Priestesshood which safeguards Priestesses and their apprentices from supporters of Seti as well as all other people who might harm innocent people. This group, known as the Sisterhood of

Silence is trained in fighting against the mind as well as the body.

Everyone who lives in an entire group has obligations to their surrounding as well as their living spaces. One of the responsibilities I have is to visit the market on a daily basis and check if there are some flowers that can be used for altars. It is my most favorite time of the day. to take in the beautiful faces of people in their individual lives and enjoy their smiles. My girlfriend, Muci, and I visit the market with each other. We love the sunny sky and the cool breezes that blow down from the mountains around us. The weather is usually comfortable enough for walking barefoot on dirt trails however, it is cool enough so to ensure that our feet don't get burned. The lush green grasses cover the walkways which make for a relaxing walk. There aren't any days that are particularly warm or cold, but all the time there's a cool breeze that inspires you to thank God for the seemingly insignificant things. It rains occasionally, only enough to provide vitality to plants typically at night.

The market is just a few steps from the holy places where we are. They are located right next to that altar Isis and connected via the underground passageway. There's nothing hidden about this. It's just easier particularly if it's showering early in the day. The altars are kept clear and neat for those who want to visit. Clean and tidy every each morning to ensure that we don't need to travel around the church with lots of people. Also, they can enjoy their own space during the prayers.

I can remember taking a trip to the market in barefoot, wearing my knee-length tunic, to look at. It's not like I've ever bought any thing. Muci and I travel to the mosque to request altar flowers, just like I had said We also talk with people, and we sing to them and offer them the blessings from Isis.

While we walk towards the temple of Isis and our floral offerings, the everyone follows us with their offerings. It's always a relaxing occasion. It is a time to worship and sing, and it is a time of peace at these occasions. They bring in more flowers, lambs or goats, dates and vegetables from their garden. Sometimes, bakers deliver cakes or breads, while women offer food or cloth for offerings. There are times when someone leaves an alcohol-based drink that is bitter, that is called beer. I like the refreshing waters from fountains however, some others loved drinking it. Yuk

The offering made on the altar are utilized regularly to nourish and assist the congregation of children and other followers in the church. When it's a great day, we always keep some for the following day, and then give the poor what we're capable of. However, the faithful are kind when they are at the altars of Isis. They understand that the sacrifices will be used to feed and help the priestesses who are in formation, as well as those in need and orphans whom we care for.

The majority people are Priestesses training. We've all been granted the sacred sanctuary from our families. A few are given for gifts to the Goddess and some sold off as slaves. We are all one to ourselves and in the eye of Isis. All of us wear lightweight tunics, and we all stroll around in bare feet. Foot covers and sandals aren't for the lower classes, or for trainees. When we get better at something, we make braids for our hair. The braids are usually embellished with white stones that is held with rawhide, grasses or any other material that is convenient. It indicates that we are getting closer to becoming priestesses who are true to Isis. The braids with adorned designs show we've completed a specific step in our study and seek to be Priestesses. The braids are not training, it's a way to learn about the goodness of Isis. This is the only way to show our love for Isis. permitted. The more braids or decorations are present, the better we're in the learning process. It's not a problem however, we do not know more about it. If anyone were to inform me that I've been mistreated or that my experience as a college student was, I wouldn't be able to believe it. There is no way to beat us. Everyone is superior to other people, however... there's the one who has a distinct style.

She's a unique person with her own persona. She isn't acting different but she is definitely distinct. She exudes charisma and enthusiasm. It's as if she has a secret that no one is aware of. We don't know exactly what it is. I doubt she has an idea of what it is. We phoned Min. Min.

Priestesses are aware that they are special even when the one thing which makes them different from us is the fact that she is the only priestess of the Sisterhood of the Silence that is with her wherever she travels. Like a body guard. She doesn't look any more than us. She's incredibly kind and quick-witted. She works as we do and rests on the floor together with us at our home. She is wearing identical loose weave shirt and walks in bare feet. However, there's something special about her. A kind of glow emanating from her face. The charismatic look that makes one want to slow down and take a look at the things she says. Min was an enslaved slave to the priestesses, when she was only one year old. The family was sick and could not take care of her. They bought Isis' blessings Isis through the gift of Min to the priestesses for the payment.

There has never been a time when we experienced happiness or evil. We've been taught about that love is a virtue, as well as the methods of birth and rebirth. But one day, that all isn't the case, because we have no clue as to how we should handle the events that are about to unfold.

The day begins with a gorgeous blue sky with fluffy white clouds skittering over the skies. The day is coming to an end with the morning prayers before getting ready for our day-to-day routine.

The Altars aren't unveiled yet, as we're cleaning the floors of stones prior to getting the doors open.

There is an instant knocking sound on the doors although they're not closed, but locked. The closest I'm to the door and I'm about to get from my seat.

Fans of Seti have demanded Priestesses from Isis to release Min. I'm not sure the reason they insist on capturing Min as a slave, but she's my sibling, and I'm fighting to protect her.

The followers of Seti are bringing large, black and dark coal. They've shaved their heads and carried large battle blades. They're fierce-looking and are prepared to cause harm if we fail to surrender to them. Min.

All of us stand firm and we don't have anything to fight about because we're not fighting. We're just a band of girls who want to shield our sisters and ensure she is safe from harm's reach even though that may mean giving the opportunity to flee. We do not know what lies coming our way however, based on what we've been taught, it is clear that we are unafraid. It's true that we are afraid of pain, but this could be a normal bodily response.

The blacks stand in the front of the entrances in a bid to hinder our way out. The Sisterhood is gathered at the foot of Isis and sings songs of joy and renewal. It is unclear what happens to our bodies, but we are aware of what our souls are heading. It's a more peaceful space and an even happier moment after this physicality has been fully mastered. When we sing, Min as she and her body guard' walk out of the tunnel that runs behind the altar.

When we sing, Seti's followers of Seti are so enraged over our courage that they demand that the black guys using axes to kill everything that stands between Min and Min.

They remove a few stones out of the floor, and create a massive hole. it's easy to create as it's made of Sand. We are arranged on the edge of the hole and begin to lash us continuously until all of us are thrown into the pit.

The piles of us are over each other and yet we are not all dead. A few of us remain living, although severely wounded. It doesn't matter as shouting would not do any good. So we sink to silence and ask God for help.

Then, the followers of Seti set the stones on the abyss, but do not fill the hole with dirt. The ones who do not die immediately will eventually die. We pray for a quick death.

Then it will be.

The scene could seem like this is an ending that's sad but we have managed to provide Min as well as her bodyguard the time to escape to the safety of. We don't know what was that she had in mind, but we only know that she had to be saved and protected because she was our sibling. As for her loss, it was not an actual death, rather a birthing of our souls to the light, authentic version of ourselves.

That's what Isis wanted to show us to start with. It was the belief that only the true, Higher Power would release us from physical chains and permit our souls to become free.

What can I take away from this?

Be true to yourself and your family, which comprises friends and people have touched you, whether physically or emotionally is the process of growing into an individual is all about.

Sadly, the fear of confined space has been a constant companion throughout my current life. I understand where it stems from and I am able to manage the anxiety that is building inside my chest. Only after analyzing my past experiences that I recognize the source of the problem. I have learned to manage my anxiety in cramped, tiny spaces, and also when there's a large number of people in my vicinity, but I've been able to focus on direction I'm going to take and what's in store for me. I can then refocus my mind from thinking about it being too small, and this greatly helped me.

I am incredibly grateful for the lessons learned in the past; they have helped me be a good friend and to trust even people who aren't worthy of the love. I trusted my own family as well as in myself. it helped my soul to be liberated to continue on my journey.

In the particular case of Della's, I was believed to be the one who killed her along with her acquaintances. When I went on my travels through the rooms of terror and rooms, she watched over me, as I uncovered more details about the incident. ....I didn't know exactly what was going on I was learning at that moment. It was only clear that I had a desire to know something more, and to find information that I had not. Della realized that I might not be happy with what I found and stayed in my mind as I rehabilitated the wounds of that specific past.

It was later discovered that a companion had appeared in the story, which resulted in three of us getting together for a third time to the merry-go-round we were aware of.

It was true that I hated having to be a mass murderer and then to kill my dear friend in the process! It was a travesty! I awoke with tears pouring through my eyes to look at Della's smiley face, offering me a hug before I had asked. Della understood that I am no anymore that person, and I would never again do something like that.

I've changed, grew and transcended the need to do harm. My soul has come great distance and I only wish that I had a tiny role in its development.

I have a lot of inspiration on Della and her work since she's taken more of a personal journey that I've. My experiences have been than a scholar of the metaphysical. I've been studying about libraries and how it functions along with the many realms and layers of them and studying my angels, guides and others in how to navigate these worlds and help others achieve this. I am learning the shamanic techniques rather than from the personal experiences that Della had. This is the reason we collaborate so well, as we view the books and library from various viewpoints.

Another instance study by Della, one that I was able to skip speaks of reliving our lessons from life as well as laying solid base. The reader is able to see the hardships of having to lead a solitary life. In the midst of cruelty, which was apparently the norm of the day. Her soul was the one who showed her ability to defend herself even now. There are many lessons to be learned by everyone here.

I was also known by the name of "the dirty one". My name I'm not sure however, this is the account as I recall it.

I recall that was in the past when we had one family out of Seville, Spain. We lived nearer towards Seville's Portuguese border than Seville however we were still located on the main road leading between Seville towards Lisbon.

Our family of four lived on one small property and allowed guests stay in our rooms, allowing guests to enjoy our basic meals and drinks. The home-brewed beer, wine as well as cool, fresh water was accessible to both animals and humans alike. The farm was a spot to unwind after an exhausting day. If there was no money to give away, we'd allow them to work at the farm or assist bake in exchange to eat and sleep. Our neighbors around us did not seem shocked by the situation and, more importantly, not to our face, however other people would scold us for permitting "paupers" to travel through and remain.

My family was well-nourished and content, and that's everything that was important to us. We could see, we performed God's will by helping other humans. The five of us. My wife, me as well as our daughters. I will always remember their faces, and the hugs and smiles we exchanged.

Like I mentioned I'm not able to remember my name. Nor does the names of my family members. I was known as "the dirty one" for many years, and I was convinced it was me and who I really was.

A few days ago, one day, a "man of the cloth" was brought to our attention to inquire about what our intentions were in our tiny farm. The person who sent him would not know, but he appeared to believe that if we were not in it to earn profits, then we're involved in something ungodly. He wanted to know what we did from our land, how we earned the money, and who was let stay, and the reason for that. What was our goal for being more close to God? It was an odd question and we could not answer it in a way we felt.

God did not disappoint us when we volunteered our experiences. We treated all people with the same respect and had only kindness from them. We treated each person the same manner God would have us treat them as if they were family members.

And then there was that one night that we didn't have anyone staying the night on the farm. That was an unusual thing to happen. The norm was at most one person in addition to the family who stayed in the house for the at night.

At night, when we all slept in our bedrooms, several the dark horsemen wearing dark cloaks and powerful silver swords, came down on us. We were dragged from our beds and forcing us to kneel the middle of the hearth. The cold stones scuffed our knees. Then we were stripped and beat of our clothes, but we didn't know why.

My wife and daughters were confined to the cart made of wood and then forced to sit with their hands attached to a wooden cage that was raised above the cart. I was pulled by a horseman, sitting or falling, with an elastic rope wrapped around my hands. This horseman was the sole authority. He pulled me along until the horses had to be rested before I was able to relax. It took days of our time and it was a good thing. I eventually figured out exactly where we were and were headed to Seville.

When we got there, I shouted to my children and wife that I adored my family and friends. I didn't know that at the time, it would be the last time I was to see or hear about their names ever again.

I was taken to the basement, according to my mind. I walked in barefoot until I was unable to long stand and was carried with my hands bound to an underground dungeon. I was unsure of the reason for my visit.

The term "man of the cloth" refers to a "man of the cloth" I'm saying this as there was a massive rosary on his waist, and the largest gold cross around his neck. He would walk up to me each day while I lay in a bed made of dirty straw. I was chained to the wall and only had enough space to stand or sit as there was no chain to lay on my back. The guy who was wearing the golden cross would stroll toward me and inquire what I did for them.

I am in a state of confusion. I'd think to myself: God and ask, is anyone else out there?

The situation continued for a number of hours, days, weeks or even or even years? It's difficult to answer since there was no light where I was, and it was impossible to sense the passing of time. I don't know for sure the length of time I spent there and my beard been growing long, white, and shaggy. The teeth and hair had left me. I was able to count each bone that was in my skin. I eventually was released from my chain and placed in a car similar to the one that my children and wife were. I was then taken to a fortress along the west coast of Spain and then to a fortress in Cadiz.

I had the ability to read and write and knew exactly the exact location of my body when we walked towards Cadiz. My mind was asking God what could they be doing to me right today. Burns, beatings, hunger, and hanging on my thumbs had not caused me to break. Was I going to break? I didn't know.

I was put in the prisons of the fortress on the coast but I was not chained nor bound. I felt the scent of the ocean at times. Sea smelled like the freedom of sea. A few other were that were there with the same conditions like me. The place was set up for the purpose of dying. It was not christian to murder us I think. In order to get us out of our plight, or the other's. They were here for entertainment. If we found anything to drink or eat, it was a blessing as there was no food and there was no water sent to us. We would devour rodents, mice insects, spiders or any other type of living thing which came in our path. In some instances, we would get so desperate that we would try to take a bite of the mildew and mold off the stone walls. If it was raining, we could gather the water and drink it when we find a way to put it into.

Once in a while an "man of the cloth" would bring me out of the room to question me about my relationship with God. My response was always the same "God knows me". They would be furious always and eventually I'd get physically detained in the prison.

At one point, we could have the full run through the dungeon as you didn't come close to gates, guards or executioners. If we did, we would be beat and then redirected to the dark, long hall towards our home in the dungeon.

Executioners did not to kill anyone, but they had a great knack of pushing people to the edge of death. They seemed to do this for personal satisfaction and to satisfy the desires to those who were "men of cloth". At times, they remove fingers, toes or other appendages in order to force the victims admit to their guilt. When you wanted to eat, you could consume what was upon the floor. This included toes, fingers feet, hands, and feet as well as lots of blood. A few were so desperate, they began eating leftovers and hopping on their stomachs and licking the blood. It was hard to imagine the way I would ever have the courage to forgive myself or be forgiven by God in the event that I did such a thing. If I was unable to accept myself as a person of forgiveness, how can God?

While the other people in my vicinity would gather those leftovers, the guards and executioners would sit on the sidelines and laugh at the pranks. In those days, doors were not secured.

I waited, and then planned the best way to get out. I was not going home. I was broken and unable to be around anyone for the first time. I wanted to go back to God. In the vast freedom and to allow God guide me to the right way back home.

Just a few minutes after I come up with a strategy, kind, three people were brought into the dungeon and beaten. Others who were in the dungeon, began to making a circling sound as the vultures. They knew that there would have leftovers as time continued and since they were starving. They had gotten habitually eating that way They would then fight with one another over the remaining food.

As the time passed and guards began to come out from the outside to observe the blood game, I was able to sneak out of to a door that was open. I wasn't sure how I was going to react, but I was for the first time in outdoors. When I let the sun's rays to touch my skin for what appeared to be the first time in my life, I realized that we were standing at the beach with a rock.

On the beach were a few small rowboats. The plan came to fruition when I sailed a boat, and, with the strength I could muster, I began rowing till I was unable to feel the ground. Then I tossed the oars onto the sides of the boat, and lay on the deck to take in the crisp air and sun. I would keep singing "God knows me", while I drifted off to rest.

God knows me. God knows me...

I think I did not wake up because God let me sleep peacefully death, finally.

As I type this post, God is still in touch with me. Still Loves Me!

What have I learned?

Another fear is that of confined spaces as well as the fear of hunger However, staying true to my faith helped me through the past and also along with my belief during my time traveling in Spain. Please don't make me believe that I do not believe in that it won't be the case. Unfortunately, my fear of the sea is still in my mind, and I am able to visit the ocean, but I don't really like the sea. I've been to Spain three times during this time and feel completely at home in the country, and Now I understand why it appears to be so familiar. I lived in the city of Seville and had a few visits and always felt like I'd been there prior to that, and I think that's what I did.

Chapter 12: The Shamanic Views

The astral plane and the akashic field, and akashic plane are all one place in my view. The astral plane is one located just over the Earth plane, and is one that is most readily accessible by the human race. It is often thought of as an upper realm from Native American tradition. It's easy to align your energy or frequency to enter. By a few minutes of practice, meditation and goal getting started, you'll be able to get going.

It is possible to access the astral by using the world tree the staircase, elevator or just by contemplating the idea. If you keep practicing your skills, the better you'll get and the less rites that you'll have to perform. Then you'll just think about it and soon get there. It's a matter of repetition and focus. Two of those things can get you a long way.

The perspective of shamanism mostly focuses on just three dimensions. The middle, the lower (lower astral) as well as the higher or astral. The three worlds are considered as alternative realities or distinct dimensions.

The realm of lower dimensions I spoke about in the book earlier is mostly about shadows, darker reflections of the realm, power animals the animal spirit totems, as well as lost souls. This would be akin to the subconscious mind and also the more dark sides of humanity.

The world above is more bright and full of luminosity. There are many things to be found in Spirit, Energy, and the route for other realities, other timelines, and planets. It's not that the lower one isn't, however, the higher realm is smaller and is easier to navigate. Humans are stuck in the belief of certain physical laws. Even when these laws are no longer applicable however, we are prone to be awed by these laws. They are a bit familiar and comfy, which is why they are needed.

In Norse mythology, the word "world tree" is the one that connects all nine worlds. The world tree in its simplest form represents the bridge that connects Heaven as well as Earth. It is the connection between God and man, and the various points between them.

Asgard - Realm of the Aesir

Alfheim - Realm of the Bright Elves

Jotunheim - Realm of the Giants

Midgard - Realm of the Humans

Muspelheim/Muspell: A fire-giant, or chaos-like force or their domain

Nidavellir - Realm of the Dwarves

Niflheim Niflheim Realm of Ice and Mist possiblely with the lower realm of Niflhel

Svartalfheim - Realm of the Black Elves

Vanaheim - Realm of the Vanir

The idea of a tree for accessing the lower and higher worlds via a passageway within its branch. The doorway is opened and you utilize the staircase, which could be one that is a normal stairs or a spiral. The staircase you discover as you walk through the door. Choose your route upwards or downwards and the staircase will come to an end on the correct point. If you're really looking to workout, you can visit the plane above and, once you're confident, you may go to the plane of ether.

Most people like to have a long hall that has an elevator at one beginning or to the other beginning of the hall. They love the excitement and the anticipation that walking along the corridor creates.

After all that it is possible that you will encounter a different kind of encounter.

This is fine too. It is my experience that I am typically ahead of most people who meditate with a guide. It is my experience that I am always ahead of everyone else. Therefore, it's okay to follow your own route towards the akashic/astral, preferable even. It is after all your personal experience, and must be unique to the person you are. Some may need several journeys until you reach an area where you are at ease in your own. Everyone is at their individual time.

There is a belief that it is also believed that the Akashic is the state of mind beyond the ordinary world; it is the God mind. Like I said in previous chapters, it is easy to imagine plugging into the cosmic USB port that is similar to that in the film "The Matrix". If visualization techniques work for you, make use of these methods. I'm not picking about anything. If something works and it does, then it is effective. Here is a suggested meditation that you can read and then test your own. You may find it helpful to take a recording of it with your mobile device and listen to it again and then take notes. Better yet...here is the YouTube link, Akashic Records Guided Meditation or if you are reading the print version; https://youtu.be/s32A8sPPYrs for the meditation I made to go with this book. You are welcome to download and use frequently the practice until you are skilled in navigating the akashic, and then journey independently.

Chapter 13: Here Is How I Start You Out

This is the version I have created of the library. Feel free to alter it to customize it to your liking. Take a look at the meditation, and have a clear idea of what you can expect, follow it. It isn't a deep contemplation, it's just to help you get comfortable visiting the library and getting be used to visiting librarians while getting an idea of the geography of the in the Astral Plane. After you're comfortable, with this, you are free to personalize your experience. Do whatever you want and discover. However, be aware of the warnings I gave you. These are to protect you, so do not try to break them easily.

The world is surrounded by God's healing, protective and loving light and no thing that could hurt you or be attached to you is able to enter the sacred spaces. Your safety and security is assured in all circumstances.

Relax your eyes and make sure that you are seated by a cushion and that you're comfortable, secure and not be disturbed for approximately 30 minutes. Visualize yourself as you stroll peacefully along an idyllic garden path. Flowers of a large size and bright color with soft velvet petals are lined every side of the pathway and are blooming in full. When you try to touch one of them, they may be a little agitated, or even rustle as a response to the contact. Take a deep breath and the sweet scent fills your senses with tranquility as well as joy and peace. The road ahead is smooth and easy to walk. It is soft on your body. Sunshine sooths your shoulders, and covers you with a soft cover of warmth and yellow. A bright blue sky draws your attention upwards while fluffy white clouds drift past like unmoved hands. The feeling of being relaxed and peaceful is evident when you stroll in the beautiful garden. A few minutes later, you will come across an elegant iron fence. The gate is decorated with colorful flowers and ribbons that bid that you be welcomed to go through. Near the gate, you find a huge blue urn, with an open lid made of glass. It is the place the place to put your worries worry, anxieties, tensions and worries. They aren't needed in this urn and should not be carried to the next person. Lift the lid of the urn, and then gently put everything you stress about and worries everything that takes up space inside your head and put them back in the Urn. The urn will be empty when you return if you choose to take them back but you definitely don't have to.

When you've cleared yourself of anything you don't need anymore inside the urn, place the lid back in place and walk to the gate. When you are walking along the path, it opens up into an area with benches made of stone as well as sculptures, lovely plants and enormous topiary filled with white and pink blooms that are in full bloom. Take a moment to relax for an hour in contemplation of what you'd like to study in the library. Make a list of thoughts in your head about finding answers in the past that had the biggest influence on the problems you are currently facing within this lifetime. This is the perfect best time to contact your guides personal for help in case you are feeling the need.

The moment is now you glance up and observe the doorway appear right in front of your eyes. A stunning white marble frame that has large golden doors appears before you. Three steps are all that you must take in order to reach those stunning golden doors, which sparkle with the light of day as nothing else you've seen prior to. It's like something that comes from the universe of angles. When you walk up to the door, they automatically open for you in anticipation of your arrival, and inviting you in.

When you step inside, the large vaulted ceiling as well as the many floors make everything appear smaller. Tables, heavy desks with leather chairs, as well as stained-glass lamps lend the vast shelves an antique look. The aroma of old ink and parchment combined with dust, leather and the oil of lamps are almost as hypnotic. A lot of books are lined up floor-to-ceiling and waiting to be put back into the slots they were assigned. Breathe deeply and smell the paper the tombs of leather, and ink. Listen to the quills as they write writing on paper or the sound of typing machines that are driven by forces not seen. An old-looking man appears and asks you to tell him what you'd like. You should respectfully ask him to view your manuscript. The author may want to know who you are or what reason you would like to read it.

Inform him that you're experiencing difficulties in a particular aspect of your life, and that you would like advice from someone you have met earlier in your life. Also, you must be aware of the reasons for having particular issues. What is the primary problem. You can also ask him ones you had formulated when you were in the park. You could see him disappearing into the library, returning with your book, or the person who brought it will do so immediately. The way they communicate differs from ours, and the librarian had an idea of when you'd be arriving.

While you are reading your book, make note how you feel about the book. What are the details on the exterior? Are they made of genuine leather? Do you see jewels in it? or is it covered in velvet? Do you think it's brightly colored or simple? If you open the book, can you go through it and read the chapters? Do you go to the page, and you will see the information on the table. What do you see? Are they only images and pictures? Do you have any idea in any way? Do you require someone to assist you? Don't hesitate to ask for assistance, whether from the library or from your guide. Spend the time that you can to peruse the book, but don't be concerned if you are unable to complete the book in a few chapters. The book isn't meant to be read everything in one sitting. A few of the information isn't at all intended to understand in any way. It is possible that some pages could even be empty, because it's not been composed in the meanwhile. It's okay but it might not have been recorded yet, or perhaps it is not accessible for your viewing. The information may be private for that particular life or completely unimportant to this existence. In the end, every existence deserves respect, as well as a certain amount of security as well. Read and scan until you're happy.

After you've finished closing your book, hand it over to the librarian in appreciation. Return through to the golden gates into the beautiful sunshine. If you'd like to take an hour or so talking to your guides or processing the information you have learned recently You are welcome to spend any time you want.

Once you're prepared, head back along the floral pathway to the gate. You will need to determine if you would like to get back your stress and anxieties that you have buried into the blue Urn. If yes, reach inside to return them, if not you can leave them there, and let the universe be there to take care of them for you. While feeling relaxed and refreshed from the scent of these fragrant flowers, return to the exact route you took to reach the library. When you walk back to your home, you're enveloped in warm sunlight. Slowly, slowly and calmly take note of the space all around you. Relax your feet and fingers. Start to notice how you breathe, feel the freshness of the air. Listen to the sound of others and the road and a radio far away, or your TV set on the other side of the room; everything that brings you back to your present in the present, right now. Once you're ready, open your eyes, grab food and take a drink before beginning your next phase.

It is a great option at this point to start writing down your experiences at the top of the Akashic plane. Write down the things you experienced in your memoir and the way it relates to your current life. This is an excellent option to record your journey and look back over the years and months to be followed and tracking how fast you have progressed. In the event that you keep on an effort to learn about your heart, its the journey you are on and how you can improve it, and thus make your life more enjoyable right now.

It's also a smart option to start the habit of keeping an account of your client's journal, even if you are reading it for other clients. We aren't making use of it to solicit blackmail However, we do use the journal to record our growth and progress in our skills. Likewise, when your client returns to visit, you are able to review your notes and track your growth while you do it.

The things you should write down would include more than just the things you wrote in your journal however, who you talked to, what they have said about them, whether they asked you questions that were not yours or even if you came across any animal. It could be quite significant especially if someone comes to you and talk with you. Similar rules apply for humans as well. world. Don't use the word"yes" unless you are aware of what exactly you're saying yes to. Similar to how you didn't just answer"yes" on the phone to an agent. The people you interact with from the other end of the spectrum will be beneficial to you or nice. That is why I insist on praying for protection.

Some dead people are lost on the streets. It is possible that they be a pleasant person when they were alive. It is not a good idea to have people hanging around your house or observing your footsteps. Others, perhaps other than humans, are abound in the astral lower plane, or the akashic sphere, so be aware of any encounters you may have during your time in the akashic plane.

Chapter 14: More to Explore

After numerous visits in the library, I've found that there are hidden rooms and a lot of librarians, all of them with an agenda. A few Librarians seem to be old-fashioned and don't want for you to learn about hidden rooms, or the things you could actually do at the library. It could be because of a belief in superiority, or simply out of love or trying to defend the library, it is hard to tell the truth is that persistence can pay dividends. Self-control can be beneficial, keeping it isn't really my thing, however I know that when it is the right time and you're looking forward to something more, a librarian who is right for you will come to your rescue and lead you to your very own room. Inside my room, I discovered the entire collection of books on me, my soul as well as my experience from the very beginning of time, which refers to my initial incarnation, which wasn't necessarily in this world.

There is no way that we are tied to earth as such. There are multiple dimensions, multiple universes, as well as many planets filled with living things. It is not necessary that we are entirely from earth, or even this one.

There were several areas in the library as well as corridors I wasn't allowed to enter. The librarian I was assigned to or the guide simply said that they were not meant for you. They were for somebody else. They aren't suitable for you at the moment. As I am able to visit any time, whether deceased or alive. Well, dead according to human standards and then. The Akashic is where the life-review takes place when we die, and it is in which we are evaluated. This is not done by God rather, by our own standards. This is in which case we will be sent in the next step of our journey or returned to learn. If we've fallen short of our own expectations, we'll be offered the chance to re-learn what we did not learn previous time that we came here. You could also be assigned to serve to be a teacher for someone else to guide to navigate their way through the world.

True, there are exceptions. Not all people who are our Spirit guides are volunteer. A few of them are given to us, whether we like they or not. Their progress to the next level is entirely on the quality of a job they can do in interacting in their relationship with us and their colleagues. What we accomplish earns the company brownie points. It also means that they've assisted us in growing and advance. They've helped us gain an comprehension of our lives and challenges; and they've benefited from the lessons of caring and giving.

Now it's the time to tell a cautionary story. I was in the library during the time that was not getting better and I decided to go to the library, to tear my book up and begin over. I banged on the door and demanded that I be allowed into. I kicked my foot in the air and informed the librarian in unambiguous words that I wasn't willing to endure this deceit any more; I needed my book right now.

I received a book and I quickly set it the book on fire. I looked him right in the eyes and said I wanted to begin with a brand new book. I desired the white leather, with a ruby at the middle. This is precisely what I got when I opened my book that was brand new and I began writing day one. I was sat there in the first day. I was unable to find anything I wanted to write, so I packed my book, then went home and finished the practice right at that point.

It is now clear that the librarian had to tolerate my actions as I was not aware what was right when I was in the library and was being considered being a child. It is now clear that this type of behavior will not be a thing to tolerate in the future. Actually, I stay away from that specific librarian whenever I visit to avoid embarrassment due to the sheer insanity that led me to throw a tantrum in initial in the first.

I have my new, brand-new book. I've actually made notes in it. I'm fairly certain that my previous book may still be there, but maybe it's a little tainted and I am sure that I was humourously accosted by this extremely stern and threatening male. It's not like I'm frightened of having another interaction with him. Be courteous at all times and show respect to any ways. These are the people who have been your elders for millions of years, and are able to know a lot more than you. Sure, there's a way around it whatever the case, there's every time you need to do things.

However, I'm not going to explain the details of that. You have to discover your own unique way for doing it. If you're looking for it hard enough, you can find it.

Chapter 15: The Rules of the Game

When you engage in meditation with fun it will make the experience more energizing, deep and more profound.

Your life will be transformed by meditation -if you allow it.

It's quite a bold claim however, if you're willing to stay with me, I'll promise to make a compelling case and you may find yourself committed to your daily meditation routine.

If you're someone who thinks it's impossible to meditate, or you're supposed to be in the lotus posture and chant OM it's a lie in both cases.

Anyone can be meditative when they grasp the fundamental principles.

All you need is a few minutes along with a cozy peaceful space.

* Commit to yourself, and keep it.

* Be as consistent as possible

* Let the experience naturally unfold.

Beware of judging you and your experiences

In the following pages, I've documented my experiences each day, including those days that life threw me off. Sure, I missed a few moments however, I did complete the task. It was definitely worth the effort.

I was in your the forefront of my thoughts, Dear Reader I took note of the mind games that frequently led me off my meditations. It can happen to anybody no matter how much practice. There will be moments that your mind is completely disorganized and it's difficult to keep track of the thoughts that are wandering. It's common.

You can do this by honoring your promise and continue to show yourself. Your time spent in this method is investing in your self and the return is incalculable.

Your guides are available, eager and ready to connect. The missing link is you. However, this can change through determination, commitment and a lot of practice. This is what the challenge all about.

Are you ready...

Pre-Meditation Preparation

Yor make an alarm set to an exact time, or simply follow whatever clock you feel is appropriate. It's up to you. It's about finding your best route for you.

Method 1

Start by connecting to Your Akashic Records using the Akasha Unleashed Access Prayer (end of chapter) Or use any other methods you're at ease with. When you intentionally connect to your Records before you meditate and meditating, you will be able to believe that the information you receive is pure love, truth, and light, all for the highest good of you.

In the initial stages of the meditation, a myriad of unrelated thoughts might be running through your head as if you were a hamster riding a wheel. It's okay, relax and be aware of the rhythm of your breathing. Be calm and don't worry about any erratic thoughts.

Say out loud what you'd like to pay attention to. You can feel the vibrating words as you speak. Let the words resonate through your mind. Make this an experience that is multi-sensory.

If you find your thoughts bouncing around at times, it's okay.

Stress, tension and strain which is counterproductive. As you would in the case of a distracted child Keep bringing your mind to your breathing or your goals to be focused on.

But don't be a rigid. When your mind wanders to the other side, let your mind to wander moment and then see the direction they take. That could be the chance you were hoping for to share something significant.

If your whole practice is centered around deep breathing and then focusing, it's all fine. You're making your way down another path that leads to awakening, where listening to your guides and angels with effortlessness is as easy as breathing. Wouldn't this be worth a little effort?

After your time is up then, express your gratitude to your guides gratitude and continue forward with your day.

Keep doing this every day for at most every few days. In time, you'll be easily able to slip into a more relaxed or receiving state.

Method 2

Start with beginning with the Akasha Unleashed Access Prayer. Next, use a recorded guided visualization that is a resonance with your. Once you have reached the end of your recording, stay in that spherical, uncluttered space that connects to the guides.

At first, allow anything that is wishing to manifest to manifest. (Having began using an Access Prayer, you can believe that the information you receive comes directly from Your Akashic Records.) When you're more proficient in your practice then you'll be able engage in a dialogue with your Akashic Records. Remember to walk first before running. Keep your cool.

Chapter 16: Toning The Muscle

As time passes, you will begin seeing more activity in your meditation in the form of visuals, physical sensations noises, or some sort of feeling/seeing words appearing within your brain. It's like watching a movie or a film screen. The experience you get is unique, therefore what you experience may not be right to the person you are.

As you continue to practice and practice, you will reach the point where you can hear your guides and angels while just going about your daily routine. You'll be amazed at the frequency they communicate by sharing their wisdom, insights amazing synchronicity, and inspiration. Daily life feels downright magical. The soul is filled with excitement and awe.

Expanding Your Experience

The act of meditating can be described as daydreaming. Anyone can have a daydream. There's a good chance you've been receiving images, meditational messages, but thought they were your self-centered thinking. If they appear from nowhere without any connection to whatever you're thinking about, it's an indication of a message.

Visuals usually begin as short flashes, or even snippets. They should be allowed to flow, and convey thanks. If you can, stop whatever you're working on and take a picture with as many details as feasible. In time, these flashes will grow. In the future, that they transform into virtual movies.

Do not try to influence the image. If an object or a scene transform, let it flow along with the change. Don't try to return it to the way it was. There's a reason for it to change. The goal is to progress using your visuals instead of tying it down. The goal of meditation is to fluidity and relaxation. It's the reason you'll feel calm and rejuvenated afterward.

When you engage in this particular type of meditation in which your goal is to reconnect to the Akashic Records and team, the information that you receive is divine in quality. This means that it's encoded by the energy of light, love and the energy of vital force (VFE) from the creator. When you practice meditation by this method it's filling your tank of energy with a dose of VFE. You may now understand why this is an essential habit to include into your routine?

After you've become proficient in connecting, it takes only a couple of moments to create a strong connection.

It takes only moments to experience a new downloading of VFE.

You Can't Ask For Too Much

If the infusion of VFE was your sole goal it would feel full. As it's connected do you have a reason to engage your colleagues? See if there's an idea or advice they'd like to pass on at this moment and/or ask any questions that you'd like.

Be prepared to be amazed when they convey a message by means of archetypes or symbols as well as metaphors. There are times when you'll receive straight-forward responses. In most cases, you'll receive responses that need some concentration and concentration to comprehend. By providing the answers this way, the team will be able to offer more than just a straightforward solution. The majority of them will add more messages. The message you receive will be clear and waiting to hear, and afterward, if you go back (you have written it down, right?) You'll usually uncover a deeper meaning that just waited for you to receive it.

It is recommended to Google any symbol you encounter. Consider your message as an enormous puzzle. The goal is to discover every piece and put the pieces together to let you know the bigger message that was in the background all along.

If you are frustrated by the lack of clear answers Be aware that your guides won't, will not provide you with the information on what you should do. It is strictly forbidden. The breadcrumbs could be dropped or give clues, as well as transmit encrypted messages. Once you have spotted or received these messages, you must make a decision on what to accomplish. Soft, kind nudging is fine, however not telling them, as it would leave you nothing more than the puppet.

I invite you to take on Metatron's 21-day Meditation Challenge. The challenge will transform how you think about life in ways that you can't imagine. And, dear reader currently, in the change that is happening to humanity You need every additional help that you can obtain. Do you want to boost your frequency and gain access to greater wisdom? The practice of meditation can assist you in this.

The best decision you could do.

Akasha Unleashed Opening Prayer

The Divine Creator is the reason, and it's my desire

to make a clear connection to my Akashic Records

Through this, only light and truth through which only light and truth will.

I need your help to comprehend your lessons and help me to

integrate them into my daily living.

Please help me put your knowledge into practice

to bring abundance and to create the abundance, happiness

and the peace that I seek.

It will be so from now on until the end of time.

Thank you Thank you, thank you.

Akasha Unleashed Closing Prayer

I am grateful to all the Masters as well as the guides.

Teachers of the Akashic Records

Thanks for their help in my search for answers.

I'm planning to return

Third-dimensional awareness.

Thank for your support. Thank you. Thank you.

Metatron:

Listen. Take note and study. What you want will be within reach. Are you feeling the enthusiasm growing closer? Are you feeling the anticipation building in your team of guides?

The true awakening. Awakening to the fullest extent. Greater awareness than ever previously. More perspectives.

More ambition. Potentially higher. More risk, but also more rewards.

Debbra: Are you really risking anything? Is that from me or from you?

Metatron LOL that was me. There is no risk to worry about. This isn't our policy nor our intention to put the risk of putting yourself in danger. Actually, when you're aligned, there is greater risk of not doing more risk in not taking action. The risk is the missed opportunities.

Debbra: (Hearing Hank Williams singing I'm so lonely I'm Going to Crying) "Hear that lonesome whippoorwill?"

Metatron: Being lonely is just a fantasy, as there are always three separate selves (ego the higher self, soul) and your whole team who are constantly busy with this errand or another in the service of your needs. Let yourself feel these feelings, or perhaps feel them. It is possible to imagine the shape and size, or in any color that you want. The shape doesn't matter in their quest and they'll happily change shape and appearance that's pleasing or even appealing for you. They are enthralled by your lively enthusiasm and curiosity.

Debbra The note to self to self: stop editing, and just note the information in the order they are displayed.

The sound of the outside is disorienting. It's okay, I tell to myself. Wait until it passes. Inhale deeply then return to the breath.

Okay, so where did we go?

Metatron The Metatron. The time is now. Where are the memories of the past.

You may be wondering: What's next? Everything! It's more than you think of in the present. What you will feel depends on you. What amount of time do you devote to these activities and pursuits? It's all in the details.

Try meditation, for example. If you make it a priority to spend only 15 minutes per day, your spiritual development can accelerate in leaps and leaps and. Speed up like a high-performance sports vehicle. You'll be accelerating like a puma at the scent of its quarry.

When you speed up, you can slow down to take in each moment. Are you able to see the difference?

Be mindful and accelerate your pace, to allow yourself to enjoy each delicious moment.

Debbra: My mind is wandering... What amount of time am I left?

Refocusing on breathing. What's next? Do we have something else? Are we done?

Metatron: (Smiling at my frustration and indulgence in my speech.) It's true that everything that is worthwhile to have is worth waiting for.

Debbra Pauses to check for pizzas baking in the oven. Darn! I really screwed up the whole thing I didn't take the plastic off of the top.

Metatron Metatron: Nothing is inherently bad that can't be corrected in some way.

Debbra: Breathe deeply, take a deep breath and let the message pass through. Oh, I smell the plastic burning. Is my pizza going to be destroyed?

Metatron: It's ok. If something is damaged, it's not meant to be. It's never too late to make salad. The fifteen minutes you have are over.

Debbra: However, I could be a bit more patient.

Metatron The Metatron says: For you to stick with the program. Soon you will see that the reason behind this.

Debbra: Okay, thank you Metatron for all your love and patience. What's up... What do you think about my question?

Metatron: They'll keep. There is no possible time.

Debbra: Did I say you did or did I?

Metatron You were the one who did it There is actually the possibility of a time line and you must to keep an eye on it.

Debbra:

Okay Metatron, I'm ready to receive the dictation.

Metatron Metatron: This is great. Let us proceed...

We are in a moment of unity. there's much chaos throughout the world. This is not surprising.

Chapter 17: Deservedly? Do you'd prefer to use?

Metatron Metatron: Yes, it is the reason is that it's karma straightforward and pure. The result of a raging storm of fear, rage as well as bigotry and hatred. These negative thoughts have been pushed to their limits, much like a car radiator that has reached its maximal pressure. The pressure has to be let go. The pressure must release, releasing an area for reconnoitering taking stock, revising priority, and considering the implications of decisions taken, whether conscious or not. It must happen just as quickly as the sun is rising.

In the present, you may be feeling anxious be sure to keep your eyes on your. Be confident. Be sure that you'll make it out of the smoke and debris from the explosion. Once the air is cleared, you'll still be standing. Believing that there's a greater source of power throughout the whole scheme.

Everything is not random.

It is not long before you can begin to see changes taking place. Gradually, other like-minded souls as well as you change towards a completely new mode to be.

More understanding, more open and more compassionate. Higher visions of yourself and a greater sense of purpose. There is no chance that you're present at the moment you are. It is an impressive design and a frame of which you, by your options, will complete the necessary details.

The result was always in doubt. The plan was always there to bring you to the place of awakening and development. Peace with love and prosperity. It is a respite from the daily grind of strife and fear. The oasis of your soul, a bit as a trip to the soul. (Big grin)

Debbra: It sounds wonderful but how do you follow it?

Metatron Then what do you do? Whichever you want to choose, of course. With the new age of technology, you'll set your goals higher. The possibilities are greater for the things you can achieve.

A lot of people will collaborate together with Gaia to purify and restore in order to restore the land in its entirety and restore good well-being.

Gaia will be the one to tell her side. Gaia will expose details previously hidden. She's been keeping these secrets safe until the time of awakening. In partnership with her, the world will be amazed by the speed at which progress can be made. Vocals will be raised with joyful song -- soothing music.

Debbra: I'm close to listening to a certain frequency, however it's blockage. Metatron Did you intend to broadcast a particular frequency? I'm hearing 1021... gigahertz(?) megahertz? Not sure. Doubtful about the accuracy of blocks are actually receiving a specific amount.

Metatron: Don't concern you with exact numbers. Most important is to look at the bigger view; understand the direction you're headed to so you can make more efforts in order to achieve that summit and leave behind turbulent seas to enjoy tranquil seas. Enjoy the calm waves with all the marine creatures. Peace and harmony among the marine species.

Debbra: Does this suggest that we'll cease eating animals?

Metatron: It's up to you to make that decision. We do not make any judgments on the matter.

Debbra: Thank you Metatron. What else?

Metatron: Namaste Dear One. Take a rest and then return again tomorrow, so that we can be able to continue the conversation. Be blessed.

Debbra:

It's late. It's a good thing I didn't have to wait for too much. Is there anyone else Metatron? Oh, that's so peaceful. Outside, the wind is blowing. Are you wondering what amount of snow we've got?

Focus, breathe and you'll be able to accomplish this. Just heard Alfred Hitchcock's voice saying "Good evening."

Dry throat? require a drink. Hot, don't have focus. This takes a long period of time... It's time changed positions, perhaps it will help. Oh, I wish I had thought of this sooner! (Meditating in the sense of.)

That's better. Take long, deep breaths. Take a deep breath... Metatron are you still there?

Metatron The Metatron whispers almost as an animal purr.

Debbra: Let's take this show going on tour.

Metatron: Patience. Keep it all at a good pace. You can center yourself. Connect to Earth since the energy will be fluctuating this evening, around this moment.

Debbra said: Okay, I'm grounded super very well.

(In an image) I imagine my youthful self riding an swing. The legs are stretched out, the torso turned back and long brown hair flowing in front of. The wearer is wearing an icy blue shift and the yellow band on top. The swaying of a large oak tree, white oak. I can hear the sound of a squeak.

(Hearing sings) Sail, sailing on the primary...

What is it that has to do with swinging? anything to do with swinging?

Metatron: Swinging, sailing The same thing, the same distinction. The energy flows and that's what's important. Relax, breathe, and let your energy flow freely and effortlessly. Relax and let it take you through its silky waves.

Debbra: Are there sinewy waves?

Metatron The Metatron: Electricity in the form of strands sure. You can flow with it like a will-o'-thewisp with no worry about anything simply flowing like tumbleweeds that make a tumbling sound.

Follow the direction of the wind you. Let loose and wild instead of stodgy and cautious. Bring back the joy and excitement of excitement from your childhood as you grew older, and before the adult burdens have taken root on your shoulders.

Debbra: That is so good, thanks Metatron.

Metatron: Yes. Just remember to remind yourself every each and every now and then. Trust your team to offer a friendly push whenever you get too overwhelmed by the worries and worries of your day. It is their right and a right.

Debbra: It's like a gentle alarm and I think about.

Metatron This analogy works.

Debbra: Which is the right name for this? Do not try to alter. Take down all the info.

What was I and we? Sliding along, like a tumbleweed. It's moving along... which is next? (From the track Tumbling Tumbleweed which was performed by Sons of the Pioneers)

Wow, it's really making noise. I'm in need of a haircut and this one is driving me crazy.

Breathe... focus... The throat is dry and coughy. A myriad of distractions... Sorry Metatron.

Metatron: (Metatron takes my hand to help strengthen the connection.) Take a stroll.

We walk along a rough gravel road, dotted with pebbles of different kinds. Trees and grass define the landscape. The air is cool and calm. Dusty puffs of dust flutter out at our feet. The temperature is warm and we head toward a bench made of wood located near a tiny stream.

While I am sitting on the bench, a huge shade tree is visible above the bench. Congratulations to the team! Making sure you have all conveniences of life before I ask for them or consider the need for them.

Metatron and me sit peacefully at the table for a while. Both of us are keeping to our own advice, as it seems. Perhaps it's an energy that is quiet and in having no pressure, but just being through the present. In this moment, my thoughts are less agitated. More prone to fancies of imagination.

Metatron: (Turns to look at me.) This is nice, isn't it?

Debbra says: I said yes.

Metatron Metatron you to take some time contemplating similar to this. You're surrounded by a lot of frantic enthusiasm, racing around, deadlines, obligations, and situations and too much giddy-up within your daily routine.

Debbra: Metatron You've handed me the task of a lifetime and I'm feeling the burden to not let you down in addition to my other commitments that remain.

Metatron (Nods acknowledging) Do you think you'll be over time?

Debbra: No, not exactly. It is true that I have the ability to delay time. Perhaps I get to much too deeply into the excitement and then forget for a moment.

Metatron: Yes. It's fine. Make your correction as soon as you realize you've fallen off from your synchronized line.

Debbra: Yes. It is time to be more mindful. Even though I agree this with other people but I too often find myself caught in the whirlwind.

Metatron: Don't judge yourself for doing extremely very well.

Debbra: Really? I'm asking incredulously.

Metatron Metatron: Sure, you are. We're glad you've made it this far, and we're quite happy. Do the best you can and make changes, and be sure not to take time to appreciate the accomplishments you have made. This is just as crucial -- if not more so as if not more importantmore so than the work itself. Be kind to yourself. A lot more kindness. More appreciation. Do not be harsh with Debbra.

Debbra (There's the sensation of close completion of the plexus solaris of mine.) Thank you Metatron. Do you have anything else to tell me about this morning?

Metatron I'm Metatron. the allotted time. We'll try this next time. At present, it's enough. We wish you peace and a great day ahead.

As if I were in a slow-motion pan away from the camera I find myself within the present. The view as well as Metatron are gone.

Debbra:

It's getting late. Today was extremely hectic in shoveling snow, and then needing to travel across New Jersey to pickup David. I was really testing my resolve to keep a regular mindfulness practice. Today, I'd feel unfulfilling if I didn't I'm making progress!

Metatron: Breathe. Watch your chest fill up with air. Notice your belly expanding with air. Keep in mind to belly breathe. The diaphragm should be stretched out. See how relaxed you feel every time you take a deep breath?

Debbra: Yep. Does that suffice? Is it time to get started? I'm feeling very relaxed.

Metatron"Hold on" and don't become so relaxed that you'll go to sleep!

Debbra: So that's the reason I'm sat up... A few more deep breaths.

Self: Discard your thoughts of all the things you've been doing in the past, and the endless to-do list. The present moment that is connected to the fifth dimension is the only thing you need. Focus. Relax.

Metatron: Ah, that's better. I've been patiently waiting for you. Glad you were able to make it.

Debbra: Me too. I'm eager to hear the next the fourth episode. What's next?

Metatron Theme: Today, let's concentrate on quietness.

Focus your attention from the outside toward the within. Bring your attention slowly towards your solar Plexus. Your attention will drift to the core in your solar plexus. relax there.

Debbra: Where are you? It's a bit noisy, as a factory industrial and booming. The sound of the pistons firing and blasting energy through, in and around. throughout. It's like the airport's air terminal. airport. Does calm actually form element of the everyday when you live in a location like this?

Metatron: It could be If you decide to create it to be so. Concentrate at the center the solar plexus. you'll begin to hear sounds gradually disappearing until you can see your self as a girl in the midst of your youth looking with clear eyes and keen senses being in awe of the quiet and purity of the energy that gentlely touches.

Connect with the human you've just met that is still a novice to the 3D dimension of reality. You can see how she's center in her center, grounded and focused within this environment? That's how she is right now, prior to being changed by the people or events. She's content to just be and soak in the beautiful energy that gives her tranquility and happiness.

Damn... hot flash! It's difficult to focus in the moment it feels like my body is burning. I'm tempted to cut off all my hair, strip it off or go outside in the snow, and reset my thermometer. At the moment, it's stuck at the 103 mark and I'm in a burning.

Metatron could you please do something regarding this flash, to help me concentrate? I'd greatly appreciate it.

Metatron: You can't fight. This delays the flash. The flash should completed quickly. In the event that you are resistant, it's that you're in a battle against yourself and make it worse. Breath, relax, allow. It's the solution, as in many other situations.

Debbra The cool has returned. That's better. The little girl that's calm, what's going on with her?

Metatron: She is a perfect example of the principle of letting go. She is not a resistance to her. It's not something she has yet learned. Her flow and joy is simply endless at each new revelation and new experience. Do you notice the tranquility and happiness? It is not a constant state of trying and stressing. With her current level of knowledge, she might be unable to understand it.

Debbra: Ok, got it. Is there something else? There's no way to connect the dots in this case.

Metatron (Chuckling) This is exactly what you want to know. The goal is to look at the top of the mountain to locate an answer. There is no answer without the question, but it's within. Take a look around to find the answers in the midst. All you require is already inside your seat of power the solar plexus. Wisdom from the past can be found in there. It is all you need to do is tap to discover all the answers that you are seeking.

Chapter 18: It's all about reflection?

Metatron: It's your reset point. If you are dissatisfied, stressed, confused, and frustrated look within. Locate your calm space. Then, look around and let the responses appear for your approval or disapproval. The mere fact that a notion is made clear doesn't mean you should accept the idea. The choice is entirely yours to make those thoughts that are a match with you and the place currently at the moment. Be assured that you won't miss the opportunity to make a difference. The offers you make will be offered once more at the next moment. Cycles my dear.

Debbra: What you're telling me is it is about trust and faith? In confidence and faith that results will follow?

Metatron: Exactly. It's really quite easy. It is not necessary to get things complicated. Be successful and go out there But first, you need for the ideas that are inspiring that will help you succeed.

Debbra: Wow, that's profound. Thank you Metatron. What else?

Metatron: Not right now. moment. Be at peace, not in pieces. This is a prank.

Debbra: It's not humorous Metatron.

Metatron: I am laughing, but You have to be on the opposite edge of the stick for you to appreciate it. Whatever. This lesson remains profoundly effective. Rethink and think about it for the duration of the next assignment.

Debbra: Thank you Metatron. #Gratitude.

Debbra:

Here it is at 11:11 and I'm only getting started yet again! What is the reason I'm doing this to me?

Metatron The Metatron says: This is fine. You are able to go to sleep afterward. Focus, breathe, relax. That's it. The tension will ease away. Remain focused on your breath.

Debbra Asks: What exciting details will be revealed in the next few hours?

Focus on Metatron and you'll learn.

Debbra Says: Yes... it's back to the present... An overwhelming sense of contentment and peace ishes over me. Beautiful, delightful, exquisite. Like everything's well in all the universe, even when it's just not.

Metatron: This is an illusion. All is as it ought to be. There's a reason and reason behind the present situation. It's part of the transformation process, which involves shedding the past to allow to the future.

Old beliefs, old thoughts and old habits... Let them go in all. Eliminate any belief which do not make you feel joyful and broad. The only thing you are doing is who is limiting the experience. It could be due to fears, a pattern that has been ingrained or lack of trust or even inertia. It's entirely within your reach to manage.

Debbra: (Ouch! Achy body due to the snow-shoveling. Focus, focus..). Was that what you were saying about limitation?

Metatron: That's it... limit. What is the reason you would choose to limit yourself in the face of the fact that the Universe is available to you? It's not a problem with the Universe. It's actually so vast it's hard to be able to pinpoint where you should begin. The answer is right just in front of you. Start by focusing on that tiny world and gradually increase the circle of consciousness gradually until you start to comprehend what unlimited feels like. There is no boundary which you haven't created your own.

There is space and freedom to expand your awareness. Be aware that your consciousness continues to grow so long as you are interested, curious and strive to grow.

You can of course decide to shut the doors or windows at any time, but we'd like to recommend that you consider expanding, because there you'll find much more of what you're seeking. More light, love happiness, peace and joy. A lot more thrills. More delicious experience. Understanding and knowing your true identity, who you truly are, as well as what you've accomplished. The things you wanted to do.

Once you've reached this conclusion, you should take note of your progress. Are you getting there? Did you make improvements? If not, then what's preventing you from progress?

If you do, how would it you feel? Are you up for more? What obstacles or blocks faced by you? What strategies did you employ to overcome these obstacles? Do you feel stuck or did you manage to find ways to get around?

We can assure us: there's no barriers you can't overcome. You're far stronger and more magnificent than you've been able to comprehend.

Massive changes are on the ways... Big!

Take advantage of the chance. Be grateful for the progress and satisfaction when you step toward the next goal. You've already reached many milestones and there's of more that are yet to be achieved. Rejoice in your achievements and see new opportunities come up to you. Enjoy wonder, joy and joy to remain your constant companions. The trio transforms a dull daily routine into an adventurous and thrilling adventure.

Are you able to recall the sensations as?

If you're in need of some analogy, this would look like a birthday party with every holiday you love rolled into one. The food is so good, you may seem a bit indulgent but that's fine. This feeling is similar to being a manna-from-heaven. It feeds your soul and enables the wind to enter your sails that will carry you onto your next great trip. Every day, there is more to discover and more joy to keep your spirit.

Debbra says: Now the energy shifts, and I sense or hear the door closing. The door is not silent, and it's certainly not loud, but the feeling of a solid, confident closure when one part is over and another starts. (What is a clever method to explain the process.)

However, this practice has ended. The time is now to wrap this conversation to settle down to get a great winter's to sleep.

Do you have a way to sign that says "off? There seems to be a sign off that ought to be. I have heard strange words but I'm not able to clearly pronounce. Do I want to come up with a word or am I communicating words using the language that I don't know?

Metatron: Relax. Do not push it. It's easy to stop. There is no need for a formal goodbye. But, if you're insisting you want to knit, we'll make formal Selah.

Goodnight and Selah.

Debbra: Thank you. This makes me feel better.

Metatron: Manana.

Debbra:

I didn't attend yesterday's event. Between an event live and writing my newsletter, making videos and going shopping, I completely forgot.

Today, I'm fighting a serious cold. Runny nose, scratchy throat with lots of sneezing and experiencing a raw. Planned Covid test for Tuesday, just to be safe. Chicken soup was made. The broth made me feel more comfortable for around half an hour. I took a few remedies, including mouth lozenges, and drinking lots of. Hope to feel better in the next day.

Onward... Damn! Every time I take in a deep breath, I am feeling like I'm about to sneeze. It is really difficult to focus.

Hello, I'm Metatron. I'm sorry for yesterday's mishap. The new routine hasn't been established until now. Perhaps I should make an alarm.

Metatron"You think?"

Debbra: I'm here. Connected and waiting to take your call.

Metatron The Metatron is very nice. (Said with a calm high voice.)

Debbra: A pause in the breath, to check if there is a sneeze. Now a coughing jag.

Metatron: slow and simple. It's possible to do it. You can take an oral lozenge. Breathe, focus, wait quietly. If you take a bit longer. Be patient. It will eventually come.

Debbra: Lozenge helped. Do we want to begin this transmission right now?

Metatron: Certainly. We're always prepared.

Debbra: (Waiting for the message) I'm sure you're aware of it...

Tips: Avoid being caught up in a hurry. If you rush, it's unlikely to last. impact.

Debbra"Fair enough.

Guides: La la la la la la la la la.

Debbra: Tuning up?

Guides: Sure, as long as you tell us so. It's more like having a good time as we wait for you to get settled in.

Debbra: Perhaps you could give it a gentle tug?

Guidelines: (Grin) It is possible to suggest that. We've got a lot of things to discuss and appreciate being able to discuss it.

Debbra says: That is similar to Esther Hicks' voice when she's singing to Abraham!

Are there any specific topics you are thinking of for the evening?

Guides: The world's yours to explore, so rise and go. (Said in a sing/song manner)

Debbra: I listened to the song's snippet before while channeling but I'm not able to identify the song. Could that be a message to me too?

Guides: If you like. This is just a reminder for the event that you've forgotten. An investigation of a few minutes may be necessary.

Debbra: Thank you so much for your reminder. I'll take care of it.

Guides: De nada

Debbra (20 mins in) I'm done...

Metatron: Excellent, now start in complete sincerity. The reason you are seeking an answer. There is a message that we wish to send. This is a fantastic situation. Let's concentrate on unravelling.

Debbra: There's a lot of many things I'd like discuss. What's wrong? Are they waiting for me to make a decision?

Do you think it's Metatron? Should I pick a subject.

Metatron: Ofcourse you can always choose. Which topic would you prefer to talk about.

Debbra: What can you tell me more about the relationship to and the Star of Bethlehem and the North Star? (At the date of this meditation December of 2020, a unique celestial convergence between planets seemed near.)

Metatron The Metatron says: That is an excellent subject.

The Star of Bethlehem and the North Star are not the one and the same star. They're different. They are distinct. North Star is ever present and is connected to Earth. It is enough, without taking other responsibilities.

The North Star is a guiding illumination. It symbolizes stability, unwavering commitment, stability, and reliability. It's eternal and secure with respect to Earth.

The Star of Bethlehem, on its own, however, has an even larger orbit, and is not seen often. The reason for this is different. It's a harbinger of a star, signalling the event of a certain dimensions. Its magnitude and size are so large that they cannot be missed. It stokes curiosity and excitement in those with more arousal than average people.

The ones who are awake are compelled to research and research, and explore, to discover this peculiarity. They'll want to comprehend the reason and significance, so they can share their understanding to others. They will be the ones to make connections to everyone else in order to help others be able to comprehend the significance behind the event.

This has been the case for a long time. Similar to how Joseph was selected to interpret dreams of Pharaoh (Biblical Old Testament tale) as well as be catalyst for pave the way for Israelites returning to their ancestral homelands and return to their homeland, so are the watchers being part of a greater plan that remains to be discovered. If the moment is right more understanding will come. Once the final dot has been set in its place, the whole thing will make sense.

Debbra: I see something like a grand cluster merging.

Therefore, the Star of Bethlehem is part of a larger picture. Is it a cog? I'm not sure how you aren't able to explain it better than this so that I'm able to understand and then inform my friends. I said I'd provide them with further specifics. The details aren't even worth mentioning.

Metatron: It is impossible to discern or comprehend the things that have not yet been revealed. At present, it's enough to be aware that the herald is the star.

What are you waiting for? Why not do some study on herald?

Debbra: Do you believe that there's a future event coming up with the importance of Christ yet we're just not quite ready to know specifics?

Metatron The Metatron. Absolutely, it's important. The details will come to light at some point. As of now, I thanks for your dedication and interest. The events will unfold and show themselves with Divine time. This is it.

Debbra: Resumption of transmission (it was as). Almost like a door closed. Due to my nose's runny and pain, this is much more than I anticipated to experience, and it's going to have to wait till tomorrow.

Thank you. Metatron could you please send healing energy to me to help us be able to make further progress in the coming days?

Metatron (Said with a soft whisper) There's nothing to be concerned about. Sayonara.

Debbra:

The last two days. I made it to the gym, but my body was busy to focus on meditation when fighting an illness. This morning I'm feeling refreshed following a long, restful sleep. The keyboard seems to be going out of alignment and I'm scheduled to attend an important meeting in the next few minutes.

Ah Metatron, Metatron wherefore art thee Metatron?

When I'm there with no response does this mean I'm not being diligent and patience? Do I need to wait in the quiet and trusting that when the right time comes appropriate, something will happen?

Metatron You're now getting it. It's easy to spot in the event that messages come through. It's not the same when you do not. Are you able to be steadfast in your vow even if you have to sit in silence to think about your thoughts?

Debbra: It was a surprise.

Metatron: Be alert, be fresh to avoid falling into a state of complacency, repeating what you think is the right message instead of really listening to the current message. It's much too easy to go back to your previous knowledge rather instead of waiting with confidence and believe that fresh information will be coming for you.

Debbra The thoughts of Debbra towards an answer I thought of. I shared the information I received and it was a bit hazy and I began to question whether my words were accurate. In the face of completely new data, there's some uncertainty. Was I able to get this correct?

However, I believe there was some truth in the story. But not all of it. This is still in the process of being revealed. Yet, new information require more thought and consideration, as well as time to process the frantic thinking that is in wait to get rid of them.

Thank thank you. I understand why it's crucial to make time for a morning meditation despite not being someone who is a morning person. It's crucial to arrive at a good state, ready to be in the clarity of a channel, not one that is sleepy.

Metatron The Metatron: Sure, and Now, you should take care of your attendees at the meeting due to arrive soon. The meeting can be resumed at a later date while you think about your new knowledge.

Debbra:

My thoughts are scattered all across the board this morning. My newsletter was sent out today, and I'm now ready to calm down. I'm working on a discipline for being still and waiting.

These thoughts are based on John Denver, who was definitely a channel which I published a piece on.

A headache is forming in my back.

The furnace started up, and reminded me of how thankful I am for fuel supply today, ahead of the major storm.

I don't have a plan, simply waiting as silently as I can to see if some sort of thing to happen.

This is a way to practice the discipline of taking the initiative, becoming comfortable with silence and allowing the guidance needed to get into.

Metatron: It can do your body and mind a lot of good mentally and physically.

Debbra has more thoughts about the pressures of family commitments. It's becoming apparent that I can focus on breathing only for long minutes.

A few fragments of thoughts. Conversations, film bits, flashing around as if I'm floating And they're floating by me.

Then, I noticed that you're not engaged. That's progress!

Hot. Have you been there for fifteen minutes already?

Yes! Done for now. It's a feeling of accomplishment to be able to fit the time in before midnight! Thank you also for reminders on the computer.

Debbra:

What can you share with me this morning?

I think this practice and the silence of it can be a sign of something bigger that requires time to express itself. It's not easy, but I'm committing to sitting silently for 15 minutes should that be what is required by me. It's a bit difficult to keep my phone ringing.

A vision appears at the roof of my head expands and I am flooded by the darkness of the sky and the stars from the universe.

Chapter 19: Does that mean being open to new possibilities?

Tomorrow will be filled with traveling and other family obligations. I'll try to relax during the evening, after I return back home.

Vision is continuing: The sky and the stars are streaming into my head through the open. The stars are flooding my senses. They're filling me up and bursting my arteries. My heart is bursting with Universal wisdom. Was that the thing I've been awaiting for?

The question is the question: how do I figure out how to collate, organize data, analyze the plethora of amount of data?

Vision closes with The folders of files, well organised into boxes. On their own, they have been compiled and are waiting for me to research start.

It was exciting and intimidating, yet I couldn't be given this task in the event that I was incapable of completing it. Now I'm able to go through the process of going through all the data and compile them into helpful reports for sharing with.

The time is winding down, it feels like the day is over. A day more of adhering to the prescribed protocol.

Thanks for the team!

Debbra:

Christmas. It was a wonderful day. It was a great day to prepare food, and get gifts prepared. This year, I decided my own best interests rather than allowing everyone to be with my personal cost. It's a wonderful feeling.

It's been a while since my last meditation. I'm still having a great time and am awake. It's just a spacebar that's hindering my breathing. Breathing, breathing, breathing.

I'm here. If you've got a message you would like to send me a message, I'm waiting.

Who will be speaking in the coming hours? Do you know who will be speaking?

The belly expands upon inhalation. It's becoming easier to relax and not cough.

Thinking about ways I'll teach this approach. Thought about a recent discussion regarding a deeper exploration of the knowledge and application of the soul's gifts.

The thoughts wander off to a myriad of autres tasks that need attention. Anything? Anything? Like a game of hiding and seeking.

Guides are not games. Purposeful exercise. The understanding and growth will follow.

Debbra What happens during this procedure? Will it increase my frequency?

Guides: It may be a possible outcomes. This method is multi-purpose and vast. Long-term benefits remain to be seen. Your success is contingent upon the determination and commitment to keep going.

Debbra: Thank you. It's reassuring. The ego is a creature that needs approval.

Guides: Yes. It is likely that you are fewer guides to use when your daily frequency increases.

Debbra: It's so great to be able to hear. The neediness can sometimes feel like disappointment.

Guides: Oh, but think about how much more powerful and pervasive they were? Be sure to remember how advanced you've come. Be aware of the point of your apex. *

Debbra: LOL, good idea and analogy. Do we have anything more to say to add before wrapping up?

Guides: Com si com sa. Out and in.

Transmission ended.

* Apex is a phrase that is used in EFT (healing method -- tapping into meridians of energy) to refer to the baffling memory loss that can occur after an individual, who has received treatment that was successful, dismisses the treatment as they've forgotten the pain they felt prior to the treatment.

Debbra:

Hi Metatron Hello Metatron! I am on Day 11. In awe of the things you've got to say this morning.

Breathing in the belly. Keep your eyes on the ball... Hoping I don't lose focus, Francesca (granddaughter) is at work on her reading assignments.

The chair you are sitting in isn't an ideal choice for meditation. Oh, those FB warnings...

The thoughts are consuming me about the upcoming podcast and what we should discuss. It's possible that by then, I'll be prepared to talk about the meditation challenge...

If I'm here can be the message start so I'm focused on it instead of running around like an athlete?

Metatron You are Metatron: What topic do you have to say?

Debbra: Everything! Do you have any more information about what we can expect in 2021?

Metatron"Slow down. Don't rush. There's still a lot to learn from 2020. Take note of your surroundings. You can find peace and tranquility in contemplation. Find opportunities to bring peaceful and bright for those around you.

Debbra How do you explain this bizarre vision that appeared to indicate that my attempts were doomed?

Metatron Metatron: That wasn't the intention. You have to take your time. Take your time and follow the breadcrumbs. seek assistance. You will find that everybody is waiting. Be confident in the face of people who might be against you. You are surrounded by the angelic armor as well as The Mantle of Light. (A donation by the Akasha, to help me in my job.)

Your light shines to others, by the light that has been set for you by others that have come before. Trust is indeed an important factor in the fresh phase of your role. We will always be by your side, helping your hand, encouraging the cause, encouraging, and whatever else is required will be provided.

Debbra: Thank you. Thank you for your help. The mission can sometimes be daunting. Who do I have to be carrying this Mantle of Light?

Metatron: It might benefit to know you're not alone?

Debbra: It can be helpful. There is less pressure to achieve perfection.

Metatron: You've worked towards this for several years. We are confident and have faith in you that you'll never falter. This is a huge obligation, and one you're ready to take on.

Debbra: What's with my family? Can they survive the next fight?

Metatron: The people who decide to remain. It is not the concern of anyone else. It's their soul's journey to take. Be focused on the journey you are currently on and allow every soul to take the same journey. Your responsibility is to spread your teachings accessible, not to dictate how they should be employed.

Debbra: I guess that in this life I am an agent of the messenger?

Metatron Metatron an exact description. As the Voice of the Akashic Records we transmit our message across the globe.

Debbra: Do you have more?

Metatron The Metatron says: It's true yes, but we'll wait. Give attention to Francesca.

Debbra:

Last night, I had vivid dreams about discernment. The theme of a huge series of dreams: Discipline is an offer to you. Make sure you choose one that is in line to your desires and goals. It's the right decision of a soul that is awake.

I am happy to have an early morning start this morning. Take deep breaths, breathe deeply into your belly...

Cinnamon pops into your mind. Why? Do you have a message that needs to be received? Is there a lesson to learn? Cinnamon... Breathe. If there's a message to convey, let it to flow.

Metatron: Plaaaayyy ball!

Debbra: Huh? I can't get settled and comfy. My arms do not seem to be able to sit anyplace. There's a lot of shaking around.

Yesterday brought such an amazing message. What's the problem with this?

Metatron"No judgment. If you can just spend 15 minutes thinking more clearly, you'll be rewarded. This is a treat to yourself. It is possible to be more than the master of your thinking that you were before. (Referencing previous message)

Debbra: I'm beginning to notice an ephemeral space of silence. That's progress!

The water is a haze of Nothingness. It is soft and relaxing. It feels like floating in the raft. A floating body that is a little cold. I am allowing myself to be pulled into any direction that will lead to a deeper understanding. It is a one-to-one experiment. (A research study that involved one person.)

Metatron: It will be for everyone who takes on the task. There will never be two trips identical.

Debbra: The smell of pine lingering across. I am rubbing my hands against a long, soft pine tree. The feathers are drawn across my face, over my eyes. Breathe...

There are a lot of questions swirling around the pine needles as well as feathers. Contrast? What is the type of feather? My eyes were shut, and I couldn't tell. Breathe...

I notice a piece of paper burning of paper right in front of me. The flames grow larger and the paper begins to break down the dark pool of water is visible to the side. Velvety, darkest blue.

The goosebumps, the cold, the cough when the furnace's blower starts but the heat needs to catch up. Then, warm is finally replacing cold.

Metatron: Cycles. The life is made up of cycles. Out, in, around. In, out, round about. As if you were the calliope ride. The brass ring never stops returning. While you're on the journey of life, it'll come to. There are endless opportunities to try new actions and produce new results.

Unknown: There's no end by you, yet, a voice yells out.

Metatron: A metaphor You are sitting in the canoe, without paddle and seemingly in the hands of fate or the elements. However, this isn't the case. Every decision you make, your canoe is pushed forward. You control the canoe and always have been. The illusion of helplessness can be a lie. You just need to be present and pause (like during a meditation) for a moment, and then you'll be connected to an array of choices of which you could choose.

If you choose wisely, you'll enjoy life with ease and happiness. If this isn't your life, you should take some taking time for reflection to discover the needs of your heart. After recognizing this, you can choose a different path and quickly and watch how swiftly your path shifts to an improved state of alignment that for you appears as effortless and happiness.

Pay attention to what you are feeling. If your travels are rough and uncomfortable decide to change your course immediately. Your canoe will reorient itself returning you to the rhythm. If you do it with calm and intent, you'll soon observe that the rough patches appear more rarely and you'll be capable of resetting your mind quicker. Believing in flow of your life will eventually become the norm, not being the one-off.

Debbra: What happens that feeling of stopping in my tracks and I'm ready to go?

Metatron Metatron the final stage of the journey you've taken to this point, which leads you on a fresh exciting and thrilling journey.

There's no need to hurry. Take your time and enjoy the experience, because the reason you're here. Take in the knowledge and spend a lot of time enjoying the immersive 3D experience that are available for you.

Debbra: Okay, so what is the connection between this and the messages from before?

Metatron The answer will be evident when you've completed your task. Be patient. There are many unaccounted for pieces to fill in this puzzle.

Debbra: Unfocused by the ideas of projects that are in the process of being completed The connection has been damaged. The session of today has concluded. It was over forty minutes.

Debbra:

Didn't get to yesterday. Today, I'm getting ready for streaming live. The temperature is too high. Stressed, thinking about it all day.

I'm in need of an email channeled prior to starting. It's not a requirement, it's a would like, I'm the one who is in charge.

Metatron can be streamed in the livestream, as well as it did before.

Debbra: Metatron does not make a convincing video if there's silence as I translate the sentences...

Ok, you're right. Trust! Breathe... Breaths from the belly. You have plenty of time. No concerns.

Metatron: Warmth and release and breathe. let the energy from the future to touch you and draw you into an atmosphere of joyous anticipation of the things you're currently making.

All of your unfulfilled desires from recent years are anticipating an opportunity to break free from the cave in which you sat in a state of stagnation. It's not necessary to postpone them or altered, however, we know that the moment when your dreams and hopes are crashing all around you, it's difficult to maintain your head above water. And even more difficult to realize what you've always wanted but was underway.

We encourage you to enjoy a huge breath, and let go of all the unfulfilled feelings and wishes. Let yourself be open to new ideas as well as new ideas and the thrill in bringing them into reality. Anything you think of, is possible to come up with. Begin with small things then move on to bigger and better ideas with confidence. It's not a matter of urgency as that could signal the presence of an unbalance. Everything happens in perfect time and is sure to delight your senses.

A plethora of delight, excitement and joy are set to go moment when you surrender to confidence, faith and the joy of your dreams, let it manifest.

It's true that you can manifest. Everything you've always wanted is just waiting to be opened the doors and be received. Take a deep breath, let it out and let it take shape in your life. The moment is now when you allow it to happen as it should.

Debbra: Distraction. The furnace is making bizarre sounds.

Metatron: Declutter. Quit talking about it, and act on it. Talk without action is just an endless stream of in the air.

Transmission ended.

Debbra:

It's late, and I'm very tired. I'm feeling a little off.

It was a great day spending time with Francesca she has lost a tooth, and was waiting with bated breath for the appearance of the tooth fairy.

Smokey, bad outdoor odor which makes it difficult to breathe deeply. I'm feeling tension. Maybe I have to accept and accept?

Deep belly breathes. You're feeling some mental fog. Affinity symptom, or Meniere's flare?

We would love to hear what Metatron is thinking about Doreen Virtue's deceitful behavior towards their love?

Metatron: It's not your concern.

Debbra: That's fair enough. A message received in a clear and loud way I be a variety of people regarding it and all of them are irrelevant. She has the right to choose the choices that work best for her even though me and many others yearn to the time she was the angel of the night. It's sad to see because she appears to be obsessed with fear and hatred for the person she used be.

Okay, Metatron can you weigh on my suggestion to produce a video focusing on John Denver being a channel?

There is no opposition towards my idea. It's now time to complete the research I've done on John and create that short video. I'm eagerly awaiting the opportunity to connect to his enthusiasm. What a fangirl. (John Denver in the Afterlife)

The sound of John sing, I'd much rather stay somewhere else, like Colorado.

What does that mean?

John Denver: No, it was referring to the song, not the sentiment it expressed. This was in the past, but it has changed.

Debbra Are you friends in the company of Jacques Cousteau?

John Denver: Of course we've had many wonderful conversations.

Debbra: Sleeping, enough to last this time. Tomorrow, I'll be back later.

Debbra:

It's me, Metatron. We can revisit the conversation concerning John Denver?

Metatron: Of course!

Debbra: Can it be okay to have access to his Records?

Metatron"Why don't we to ask him?

Debbra: I'll. We wanted to speak before I do so.

It was simple. What else would you like to share with me about your new project, a 21-day challenge to meditate?

Metatron: Let it flow let your perception of the specifics to shift in the right direction as you move. The details you are looking for aren't important to get right at the time.

Debbra: You've mentioned an assignment to fast. Would you like to provide any guidelines? prefer me to follow?

Metatron: Yes.

Debbra: I'm surprised by that. It's usually done the way you want to. Could you clarify the rules? Can I continue to take my first class next Monday morning when I return with Francesca back to the house?

Metatron The answer is that it's enough. The sooner the better however, allowances could be created.

Debbra: What is the duration of duration? What's the ideal goal? (Big boom baa boom drums sound.)

Metatron: Thirty Days.

Debbra: Everything is fine. What is the best way to use to use only liquids? Water and tea? It's a feeling I have within my body. Therefore, the 30 days of liquid fasting will be. *

I am grateful for the chance to fine tune my senses and get more information faster.

When it comes to data, Metatron could you inform me more details about this assignment for research? Do I need to create an ongoing study routine or access to data and then be able to access data as I need it?